The Replacement

The Maturing of an 18-year old in WW II

Robert F. Kauffman
"D" Co, 36th Armored Infantry Regiment, 3AD

Introduction

Much of the success of the U.S. Army during World War II was due to their well organized system of replacements. As men in the front line units were injured or killed they were replaced by other already trained men, thus keeping each unit continually at near full strength. The U.S. was the only country to do this effectively, a fact which impressed even the Germans.

Bob Kauffman was one such replacement. He landed in Normandy on D-Day+10 (June 16, 1944). A few days later he joined the 3rd Armored Division, 36th Armored Infantry Regiment, Company D, 2nd Platoon, 3rd Rifle Squad when a man in that unit had been killed. He was with that unit only a few weeks when he was wounded on July 10th and sent to a hospital in England. He rejoined his unit at the beginning of September and fought with them for several months until he was wounded again. He later joined them for a third time shortly after the surrender of Germany.

Foreword

Most books about the Second World War outline various strategic situations and then go on to describe the tactics employed by both sides and the resulting battles. The picture is usually viewed from the top down and one is rarely able to appreciate what it was really like for the individual soldier involved in such conflict. This book is quite different. It shows the reader the raw material from which history is made and describes, often in brutal form, the tedium and misery of sitting in a foxhole in the freezing cold and the intense mixture of terror and elation of being involved in close combat. What is even more surprising is that it was written by a draftee who, as a member of an Armoured Infantry Regiment (AIR), had been wounded twice before he was nineteen and who ended the war after nearly three years service still as a Private First Class.

I first met Bob Kauffman nearly twenty years ago (20th March, 1993) when he was revisiting the battlefields of the Belgian Ardennes and I was carrying out research in the same area. They say that people of similar character immediately get on and so it was with us for we soon discovered that we had both been infantrymen. In my case the selection officer interviewing me when I was just eighteen expressed great surprise when I told him that I wanted to join the infantry; "I've never met anyone who *wanted* to be an infantryman before!" he told me. In Bob Kauffman's case, despite being taught by a World War One veteran and reading everything he could about that war and the horrors of trench warfare, he developed "a very strong affinity to the infantry" and "just felt that this was where I belonged". This is all the more surprising because he came from a family with a Mennonite background and a strong pacifist attitude. He got his wish though and after training in the States and the UK he landed in Normandy soon after D-Day and was assigned to D Company of the 36th AIR. Despite being wounded twice in the same action within a few weeks of joining, he was able to return to this same Company, enter Germany with it in late 1944, only to be wounded again in January 1945 in Belgium. After recovering yet again he was involved in a serious traffic accident and received a Disability Discharge from the Army in August 1946.

This book takes us through the dramatic and often disturbing time of Bob Kauffman's service. It is written with obvious sincerity and gives us a very clear picture of what it was like to be a 'grunt' in battle and to actually close with and see the faces of the men you are required to kill or capture. Few books have done this with such clarity.

Major General Michael Reynolds, CB, ret. British Army, former commander of NATO's Allied Command Europe Mobile Force

Acknowledgments

The writing of this book would not have been possible without the contributions of many others.

From my earliest writings, my dear brother-in-law Gerald Schlonecker insisted that I go about having them published. At the time I didn't think them worthy, nevertheless he persisted relentlessly and now his persistence has been rewarded.

George Sampson was my closest companion in combat and we shared many terrible moments together. He had become a very dear friend, this noble and decorated soldier. George came from a close knit Greek family and greatly honored me with the statement that he thought with what we had been through together, that we were really closer than brothers. Some of his exploits are recorded in this book.

Vic Damon is a Cold War Veteran of the 3rd Armored Division and is webmaster for the Division Web site 3AD.com. He has been an invaluable friend and a great asset in preserving the 3rd Armored Division history.

Andre Hubert is a Belgian historian and has become a valued friend, spending hours with me in search of places where I had been in combat. He is an important presence in the organization CRIBA, dedicated to the preservation of the history of the liberation of Belgium.

Eddy Monfort, another dear friend, is a proven historian, despite his youth, and will without doubt be a great contributor in the accurate presentation of Belgium's history in the Second World War.

Gerard Gregoire of La Gleize, another valued friend and recognized historian, was of great help to me in searching out places where I had served in the Battle of the Bulge. His vivacious daughter, Marie-France, is a most delightful friend and a great help with any questions one might have in matters historical.

Roger and Renee Burnotte and Jose Burnotte; Roger and Renee own the Hotel, le Val d'Hebron. From my very first visit in 1983, they have become the most wonderful friends and it was there that I met Jose and spent much time with him. In fact the entire Burnotte family extended great warmth to me. But it was Roger and Renee who made my stays in Belgium the great success that they were by providing such beautiful accommodations. They have treated me like family and I also love them as family. My deepest gratitude goes to Roger and Renee and their lovely daughters, Katrina and Natasha.

Mrs. Gabriel Lonchay, or "Mrs. Gaby" has been a dear friend. It was in the foundation of her house where we spent most of the terrible Christmas night. It was she who arranged the ceremony for the presentation of the American flag to the village of Grandmenil on behalf of Darlene Wertman, whose father was killed on Christmas night. She also arranged a Thanksgiving Mass in my honor before the presentation of the flag. Unfortunately she is deceased. I refer to her as "Mother Belgium" because of her kindness and generosity.

I was embarrassed when my good friend Raymond Goeme told me that he had given some of my writings to Major General Michael Reynolds. However, I was highly honored after meeting the General in La Gleize when he used excerpts from some of my articles in two of his books. In July of 2008 I received an email from him in which he strongly urged me to have my writings published. That was all that I needed to then give publishing them serious consideration. My lasting gratitude goes to General Reynolds for his encouragement. His greatest strength is that he is a Christian gentleman to the core.

Three German historians have been of great assistance to me – they are Gunter von der Weiden, Timm Haasler and my departed friend, Hans Zeplien. These three men dedicated themselves to painstaking research in order to record history accurately. Hans Zeplien had commanded 14 Anti-tank Co. 12VG Division. There were also three families in the village of Scherpenseel that opened their homes and hearts to me to cause me to find them so endearing – the Artz family, the Esser family and the Rehfisch family, but especially Otmar Rehfisch who has become an invaluable friend.

Alan Fleming has been a traveling companion during five trips to Europe. His first visit was in 1990 when he, along with Pete Derr, joined me to visit Belgium and Germany. Alan had planned to video the trip in preparation for a documentary about an article called "The retaking of Grandmenil". As producer, it was later shown on Channel 69. It seemed that every trip we made exceeded our expectations. We were totally compatible in every aspect of our visits.

It was such a blessing to have two such gifted men as Alan Russell and Alan Fleming responsible for the production of this book. It was Alan Russell who came to me out of the blue with the proposition to print this book. It was Alan Russell using his God given gifts so unselfishly, who worked tirelessly in compiling and editing this work and then using the photographic skills of Alan Fleming to enhance the written word.

But lastly my tribute to my own family: My dear wife Gertrude endured my nine trips to Europe without her, in spite of the terrible loss of two brothers in the war, since the pain still lingered. It was then up to my children Richard, Marjorie and Alan to keep up the home front while I was in Europe. I give them my undying love and gratitude. It pains me deeply that my dear wife cannot be here to share this moment, since her home-going on December 26, 2008.

Robert F. Kauffman
Emmaus, PA

Table of Contents

Part I – Service

The Twilight of Innocence

One of the gifts of life as we entered our mid-teen years was to see life begin to blossom before our eyes. Another important gift was to have good friends sharing in the interesting, sometimes bewildering, but always exciting experience of the blossoming.
I was fortunate in that I was surrounded by a small group of friends, enjoying good fun as well as serious matters that we weighed and discussed. We went hiking, bicycling, or just walking downtown after the Sunday evening service. After all, the church was not only the center of our religious activities, but also the center of our social lives.

Sometimes after the evening service we would simply gather around the piano to sing and attempt to write our own songs, or even venture into writing silly verse. It happened that a number of us had the same English Literature teacher, Mr. Benfield, a real disciple of William Shakespeare. He compelled us to do endless memorization, for which I shall ever be grateful, and we had John Milton, Oliver Goldsmith, Shelly, Lord Byron, some Tennyson, and of course "The Bard", as Mr. Benfield referred to William Shakespeare – so that put us into a poetic mode. For all of this, it was Mr. Benfield who had the greatest impact on my young life in my education.

War!

The father of one of the young men in our group permitted him to use the rather ancient family car. We would all pile in and go riding through the countryside, and again, singing would be the theme of the evening as well as the usual teenage banter.
The morning of December 7, 1941 was just another ordinary Sunday morning. This particular Sunday was Communion Sunday and since our church was part of a three church circuit, the service would be held in our Macungie church. Then came the thunder bolt: Pearl Harbor had been attacked! Throughout the nation there was absolute shock that the nation of Japan would have the cowardly audacity to attack the powerful American Naval Base. There was great outrage and the call for immediate revenge.

The evening service that Sunday was a very sobering time, especially for the ten or twelve of us who were in the ages of sixteen to eighteen. We had no illusions as to what the future might hold, but among most of us there was a strong desire to do something, anything to combat that dastardly foe that had so damaged and even humiliated us. There were some of the young men who were in their late teens or early twenties, contemplating enlisting in one of the services. One of our young men, Cleave Yeahl, had already enlisted before hostilities had begun and I greatly admired him, especially since he had joined the Cavalry.

Our nation had been sitting rather comfortably by while Hitler ravaged Europe and the British Empire stood virtually alone until he made the foolish miscalculation of attacking Russia. I remember my brother Warren and I following the war in Europe very closely, since we were both history buffs. We would even strain to listen to Hitler in his rantings that were carried by some of the radio news services. And even though the attack on Russia added more grave concerns, the two oceans had given us an unwarranted sense of security that rapidly disappeared with the attack on Pearl Harbor, robbing us of our powerful fleet that gave credence to our reliance on the two oceans to keep us safe and secure.

There was a great patriotic fervor that swept the country. There was probably a unity of purpose that our country had rarely seen. Almost immediately a militia was formed known as the Pennsylvania State Guard Reserve. Since the lower age was 16, I was able to join, along with my brother Warren and a friend, Orville Gehman. We met in an abandoned church building that was owned by the American Legion. The spacious auditorium was an ideal place to meet and also to do some close order drill. We purchased our own uniforms and were issued rifles that must have dated back to the Spanish American War, but they served the purpose.

There was one insufferable part of our military training and that was to endure the mandatory reading of the Articles of War: An endless litany of do's and don'ts. Our officers and non-coms were all veterans of the First World War, and by and large were very capable. There was one officer however, who was pathetically inept and you could see the smirks and annoyance on the faces of some of the non-coms and fellow officers during the moments of his blunderings. However, it was rumored that it was his political power or some other form of leverage that made it possible for him to keep his command.

We would go on brief field exercises in the nearby areas with squad movements involved, but the only official duty that we performed came about when ration books were first distributed. It was our responsibility to guard the distribution stations. I was a member of the organization until I was inducted into the Armed Forces in November of 1943. I thought that it was a useful experience for me since I always had a great respect for our Military.

There was another organization that was quickly formed and that was the Aircraft Warning System. A small shed was constructed on the roof of the Lincoln School Building. Every plane that passed nearby had to be reported to the 1st Fighter Command in Philadelphia. The code for the call was X-ray 069. The plane had to be identified as a single or twin engine aircraft, the direction and whether it was low or high. What made it extremely difficult was that there were two railroad lines that ran through Emmaus making listening for the sound of oncoming planes difficult. Winter time was especially trying because of the high winds that would sweep across the roof with bone chilling, penetrating force. Fortunately, there was an oil burner in the shed where we could recover somewhat from the cold.

It was my brother-in-law Ed Stortz who got me involved in the program and our schedule called for us to serve on a Saturday evening from 8 to 12:00. Ed usually came fortified with a box of Cheez-its and a supply of Gingerale. It wasn't long before my future brother-in-law Gerald Schlonecker joined us so that there was now the possibility for relief when necessary.

In school, the subject of the War was all consuming. In our English Literature class, Mr. Benfield would always begin the class the same way, since, at the end of the preceding class, he would throw the windows wide open, no matter what the temperature outside, and that was sure to wake everyone up. There were about six of us guys who sat in the row next to the windows and he took particular delight in tormenting us. He would start in the rear and one by one he would run his hand through our hair pushing it down over our faces. This seemed to amuse him. He would usually begin the class with a critique of the war and at the time there was still heavy fighting on Guadalcanal. It was important to us since some of the young men who had graduated ahead of us were fighting there. Mr. Benfield had been a veteran of World War One.

One morning after his usual opening ritual he came down the same outside aisle, making remarks along the way, but for some reason and to my great embarrassment he paused by my desk and said, "none of us knows what this young man might have to go through yet." In later years my embarrassment yielded to haunting wonder. Why did he say that?

1942 was not a good year, with very little good news. There were many defeats suffered by the Allies in almost every theater, and the realities of war were coming home with the appearance of casualty lists in our local newspaper. The Draft was in full effect and men were being called up regularly. It was also the year that a good neighbor friend and I travelled to Philadelphia to enlist in the Merchant Marine Service. We were quickly informed that without our parents' signatures we could not enlist since we were under-age. We returned home very dejected, but at least we tried and how thankful I was ever after that we did not succeed.

The year 1943 was a very tumultuous year: In January of 1943 two of my closest friends and members of this small group of young people had their 18th birthdays. That meant reporting to the Draft Board to register for the Draft. The next step would be their notification when to report for their physical examinations. If passing, they would then be informed as to when they would be leaving for induction into the Military. Of course, both young men passed and their departure date given. The last night before they left for the Military, after the evening service, we walked down town as we had on many other occasions; however, this night, for some reason we ended up in the shadow of the railroad station from which they would be leaving. It was there that we said our painful farewells. When we separated and as I walked home, the painful farewell meeting lingered with me and by the time I arrived at home, I had framed these words,

> *"That spot of ground where we all bid God-speed,*
> *Today bears no flower, not even a weed,*
> *For that tear soaked soil chokes every seed*
> *That tries to erase the prints of our feet."*

How tragic that all of the joy and exuberance of our youth should be shattered by the ugliness of war and that one brief moment of our youth would always remain in our minds as the twilight of an innocence that we would never again recapture.

Enlisting

In June of 1943, I graduated from Emmaus High School and on August 7th, I had my eighteenth birthday. Of course I was eager to present myself to the Draft Board to register for the Draft. In September I received notice that I should report for the usual physical examination. The government had purchased an abandoned school house in the lower part of Allentown and this is where the examinations took place. My appointment was for October 11, 1943.

I had one great fear: In the fifth grade I found out that I needed glasses, particularly because of a weak right eye. During meals I was to wear a plastic piece over my left eye in order by use to strengthen the right eye. The fear of failing the eye test really frightened me since I was determined to get into the Military, because I didn't want to be left behind at home with both of my friends gone in the Military.

On October 11th, the old school building was full of men there to go through the examination process. Finally the time came for the eye exam. It happened that the line was so long that it snaked around the room. Fortunately, at one point the line came within a few feet of the eye chart. I quickly memorized the bottom two or three lines and when I stood at the prescribed place by the examining doctor, I rattled those lines off without error and passed with flying colors.

What a proud moment it was for me when everyone was gathered together in this large room and the names of those who had been rejected were announced and thankfully, my name was not among them. Those of us who then remained were told that we would have to take the oath required of the Military. To raise my hand and repeat the oath was one of the great moments of my young life. We were then informed that on November 1, 1943 we would report for induction into the Armed Forces. We would be leaving the

Emmaus railway station at 11:45 that day. Of course after the exam and the swearing in, I now had a more painful responsibility facing me and that was to inform my mother and father of my acceptance into the Military. As might be expected the news was devastating to my Mom. There were five sons in our family ,the two eldest sons, Charles and Clifford , were married with families, the third son, Alton had died at the age of 27 and my older brother Warren had some serious health problems from his early youth and so had been rejected for military service.

Our family belonged to a small Protestant denomination with a Mennonite background, decidedly Pacifist in doctrine. Our Pastor, Pastor Hertzog would take us aside and lay out the reasons for that particular doctrine. He urged us to apply for a Conscientious Objector status, but there was absolutely no coercion and for that I applaud him. My generation of young men with only two exceptions in our congregation could not abide by that doctrine.

There were two young men who did abide by the doctrine. One young man, a very good friend and I stood on the corner of 5th and Chestnut Sts. in Emmaus, one Sunday night for at least two hours while he outlined his reasons for going C.O. He was a very bright young man with many persuasive arguments but his position was not that of using cowardly sophistry to buttress his argument for going C.O., but they were truly the reasoning of a very honest and dedicated young man. I have always held that man in the highest esteem. I must confess that I would rather be shot at than to have endured what he and other Conscientious Objectors had to endure. There was often great hostility toward them. The other young man, equally dedicated and totally honest, applied for a Non-Combatant status and was assigned to the Medical Corp.

My dear Mom pleaded with me to accept the C.O. status and it was equally that she did not want her son to go to war, but she was also constrained to abide by the Doctrine of our church. It was heartbreaking for me to disobey my dear Mom in this matter, but neither could I violate my own conscience. No son every had a more Godly and God fearing mother as I had. She was indeed, a woman of prayer, a woman with only a third grade education whom I've said could see farther on her knees then some theologians could see standing on their tip-toes.

The next few weeks would be spent in saying farewell to friends and family members. I was living a life of high excitement, however, one evening I came home rather late and sat on the swing that we had on our side porch. There was some high ground that separated us from the city of Allentown; nevertheless, we could see the glow of the city lights, especially the tallest building in the city, the PPL building. The top floors of the building glowed red from the flood lights that illuminated it. I sat on that swing, I guess mesmerized by the sight and for the first time I seriously contemplated the possibility that upon leaving for the Service, I might never return home again. It was a very sobering moment.

When November 1st came, the four of us, my Mom, my Dad and my younger sister, Florence, or Dolly as we called her, walked to the railway station and found that there were seven of us who were leaving for New Cumberland, the Induction Center, near the state Capitol, Harrisburg. It was a painful goodbye for my young sister who would now be the only child left at home. Each of the new inductees had a small hand bag that we were required to bring with us in order to return our civilian clothes home. There was an entire contingent from the city of Allentown already on board and we would make more stops along the way.

Training

When we arrived in New Cumberland, we were marched to a building where we immediately began acquiring our clothing and other equipment. I remember being assigned an upper bunk in my new environment where, from now on, regimentation would be the order of the day and even the night. The next day, the endless battery of tests would begin. One that I really disliked and had no interest in was radio – listening to the Morse Code until it almost drove me nuts. The dots began merging with the dashes until I just gave up in despair. After the tests we were ordered to get all our equipment together in our duffle bag and march to the railway station. We were quite surprised when we boarded the train to find a dining car as well as a Pullman car among the passenger cars. We were also informed that at meal time we would eat first, and then the civilians. We were also astonished to find out that each of us had a berth in the Pullman Car. We thought, boy, this army is really great – a thought that would slowly erode.

Because of the war emergency, war supplies and material had priority on the railway system and that meant that our train would be put in a siding to let the priority trains go by. But there was no mistaking that we were heading for the Deep South. Finally, about the third day, we noticed that we had passed Jacksonville, Florida, and then not too much later we came to another station and emblazoned in large letters over the station was I. R .T .C. In smaller letters was Infantry Replacement Training Center. There was a chorus of sighs and groans when the word Infantry was seen.

In High School, I would spend time in the Library, reading everything I could about the First World War and, as horrible as the trench warfare was, I developed a very strong affinity to the Infantry, indeed, Infantry was the "Queen of Battle", so when I saw the word Infantry, I just felt that this was where I belonged.

When we were ordered to "fall out" and form in front of the station, there were other groups of soldiers passing nearby. They all looked so smart in their uniforms which they knew how to wear properly and, with their deep Florida tans, they all looked so soldierly. We must have been a very sorry looking lot with our Northern pallor and wearing uniforms that we didn't know how to wear properly. We must have looked like a preamble to a Three Stooges movie.

A group of us soon found ourselves in an area identified as Co. D. 213th Battalion of the 66th Regiment. We were assigned to our barracks which were pathetic sheds, holding twelve men each. We were alphabetically assigned with the letters of 'J' and 'K' in our hut. We also found out that we were in a "Heavy Weapons" company, majoring on the heavy .30 caliber, water cooled machine gun and also the 81 mm mortar. Of course, since we were Infantry we would of necessity become very familiar with the M1, Garand rifle. I had read and heard so much about that rifle that I could hardly wait to get my hands on one. The day I was issued mine was a memorable day. Of course it was covered in Cosmoline as a protective measure and that had to be cleaned, but by the time we had finished our Basic Training, that rifle became like an appendage.

We trained endlessly on the M1, it seemed that we would never get to fire it, but that day finally came. Since my left eye was my master eye, I had to fire left handed which meant that the spent, hot cartridges would often land on my right arm and that would be downright painful – but I didn't care, I was firing the M1. When we were finally on the firing range, I did alright and only missed sharpshooter by one point. However, on the range I was assigned to the job of latrine orderly and, since the urinal was blocked, I was ordered to tell everyone who used the latrine, officers and enlisted men alike, that because the urinal was blocked they would have to "squat to pee". What an ignominious job!

Our next mission would be to tackle the Browning, heavy, water-cooled .30 caliber machine gun – a much more complicated piece of equipment than the M1. We had to know every moving part and learn to quickly assemble and disassemble the machine gun before even thinking of firing it. Because of the intensity of the training, I would actually dream about it in my sleep. But the day finally came and I really enjoyed the experience of firing such a powerful weapon.

One day we were firing a mission: We began on a hill and fired at a target several hundred yards away and this was a competitive activity between squads. We would then break down the machine gun, the receiver and the tri-pod, and then of course, the ammunition cans. We would then move forward, set up again, fire again, and break down the gun and move another few hundred yards. At that point we were to break down the gun and return as quickly as possible to our starting point to establish who had the best time record.

At this time, I was a thin eighteen year old, but when I entered Basic Training, I was determined not to fall out of any marching formation or any other strenuous training. I decided that if there was a man in front of me, if he could keep going, then I would too. Fortunately, in our youth, my brother and I would run, no matter where we went. To and from school, or to and from church, we always ran, rarely walked. That came in good stead in our training. We had one man in our squad, a very well built young man whose name was Charles, but he was a real cry baby, always complaining that things were too difficult. This time when we finished firing the mission, when it came time to break down the machine gun to the receiver and tri-pod and run back to the starting point in the competition, he said he could no longer go on. We were all tired, but I became so angry that I picked up the tri-pod, with receiver still fixed on top of it, threw it over my shoulders and began running back to the starting point, which included running across a log thrown over a small pond. Time wise, we did real well and the company commander commended me for what I had done. I never stated that what I did was out of sheer anger because of the coward we had in our midst and I didn't want our squad penalized because of the "cry baby".

After completing our training on the machine gun, we moved on to the 81 mm Mortar. It was a powerful weapon. It broke down in three pieces: The base plate, the tube and the bi-pod. It was the most awkward weapon to carry, especially the base plate. Again there was much instruction before we fired the weapon. The Mortar has a very steep trajectory and it was always fun to see how many rounds we could get into the air before the first round hit the ground.

Our training would conclude with two weeks of bivouac. We hiked about twenty seven miles to the first bivouac area and spent time firing the M1, the machine gun and the 81 mm Mortar. We then broke camp and hiked five miles to the new bivouac area. When we arrived at the new area, a Colonel drove up in a Jeep, called the company together and informed us that he had checked our old bivouac area and found an unburied cigarette butt. We were ordered to march back to the old area and to bury that cigarette butt. We suspected that this was just another ploy to get us good and angry for some stupid purpose. In that he was successful.

After another week of firing all of our weapons we would then prepare to return to camp. That would mean a thirty two mile hike with full field packs, our steel helmet and of course our rifles. It would be a real ordeal, but how great it was when we would finally see the water tower of our camp in the distance and when we arrived back in the camp to remove our full field packs and take off our shoes it made us feel so light that we thought we could have flown away.

There was a concluding full dress parade as our final graduation exercise, and what a wonderful feeling of achievement, coming through it and now looking like soldiers and feeling that we could lick the world because of the great physical shape that we were in. We were given a seven day "delay enroute" and were then to report to Camp Meade, Maryland. While training in Florida, I developed a visceral fear of being send to the Pacific Theater, for some reason I had that great dread. It would be at Camp Meade where our ultimate destination would be determined. When we were not issued khaki uniforms, we were convinced that we were heading for Europe, or in military terminology, the ETO, the European Theater of Operations. I was really excited and delighted.

The week that I spent at home was very revealing as to how differently I felt. Those seventeen weeks had really dramatically changed me. Foolishly, I was now eager to do what we were trained for, to meet the enemy.

From Camp Meade, we travelled to Camp Shanks on the Hudson River and after a few days there we embarked on a ferry that would take us to a pier in Brooklyn where we would board a large cargo vessel, the "Sea Train Texas."

Just a year earlier that small circle of friends had stood in the shadow of the railroad station where we said farewell to those two young men: Now, as I stood on that pier with the 'Sea Train Texas' towering over us, little did I realize that I was experiencing the last flickering ray of that cherished twilight of innocence that would finally be extinguished among the hedgerows of Normandy.

From Brooklyn to Cardiff

An untimely snow was falling in the bleak, cold morning of April 6, 1944. Huddled on a cluttered pier in Brooklyn, a small contingent of soldiers awaited embarkation. Standing among bulging duffle bags and stooping under the weight of full field packs, we looked with some amusement at the mysterious numbers scrawled in chalk across the front of every steel helmet.

Above us loomed the enormous superstructure of the S.S. Sea-Train Texas, like a huge, gray, docile behemoth, tethered quietly to the pier by several scant hawsers. As an eighteen year old from a small town in Pennsylvania, this was the closest I had ever been to a large ocean-going vessel, aside from the time in 1940, when,  while going to the New York World's Fair, my family passed close by the burned-out hull of the French luxury liner "Normandy", lying on its side in the Hudson River.

After a considerable wait, we finally made our way up the gangplank to board the ship. For me, this was a rare moment of excitement, despite all the ominous portents of the nature of the times and our mission. I also felt an element of great relief in that since we were leaving from New York Harbor, we were most certainly heading for the European Theatre. For some reason, I had a strong undefined dread of going to the Pacific Theatre.

Once on deck with our backpacks and our duffle bags, we wiggled our way through a hatch, into a passageway and then down a stairwell to a lower deck. Again, we squeezed our way through another hatch and into a cavernous area with a low ceiling. This very large room was filled to stifling fullness with triple-decker bunks. A company of at least one hundred men would be occupying this limited area. Finding my way up an aisle, I selected a middle bunk. Removing our packs in the narrow area meant elbows in everyone's faces, besides tripping over duffle bags clogging the aisle. It was not an ideal place for the claustrophobic. After opening our packs and fixing our bunks, each of us was able to secure a small island of order in that sea of chaos.

Our boarding the ship must have been the last order of business before departing. Not long after we were reasonably situated, the ship trembled slightly as the great engines below deck came alive with the sound that would accompany us the next twelve days and nights.

At mealtime, we were ushered through another hatch to a large adjoining room that would be the company mess hall. We would not be seated at tables; instead, we would stand at narrow, waist-high counters that would accommodate the width of one tray. In an alcove, off to the side, was a kitchen that gleamed with stainless steel equipment. The meals issued from that kitchen would make us forever envious of the men who served on that vessel because of the quality as well as the quantity of the fare.

After our first meal, we were kept in place while an officer force-fed us with a whole litany of restrictions, prohibitions, and limitations that would literally confine us to the sleeping area, the mess hall/day room, and the deck on the stern of the ship. (Since the vessel was primarily a merchant vessel and not a troopship, the restrictions, although unpleasant, were understandable.) We were then instructed to don our life vests and make our way to the top deck where we were assigned lifeboat stations. Lifeboat drills from the first day would be an integral part of our daily routine.

It was quite obvious from the very outset of the voyage that because of the severe limitations of movement imposed upon us we were facing a monumental siege of boredom. The sleeping area, because of crowdedness, was so dark during the day that, unless you had an upper bunk, reading was almost out of the question. The middle and lower bunks were good for sleeping or simply lying there, contemplating the canvas of the bunk above you. On deck, every open area was filled with amphibious landing craft, lashed fast with heavy chains with only a narrow area left clear by the rail as a walkway.

The day room offered some hope, initially. There were a few tables and chairs positioned close by a series of shelves filled with quite a number of well-worn paperback books, which constituted a library. A lone piano sat benignly in the corner, and several men with playing skills went to it, but after fingering several chords and discovering that it was painfully out of tune, with several stuck keys, they quickly abandoned it. There was, unfortunately, one man, undaunted by the severe disabilities of the instrument, who literally commandeered it.

Armed with one song, that for some reason obsessed him, (whether it was the melody or simply the timeliness of the words, we didn't know), but "Shoo Shoo Baby, Don't Cry Baby, Your Daddy's Off to the Seven Seas" would haunt us as relentlessly as the sound of the ship's engines. Whatever other ditties he might unmercifully flay, "Shoo Shoo Baby" would ultimately end up reverberating around that steel vault with deafening sound. Undeterred by the stuck keys and treating the loud pedal like an accelerator, he kept the pedal pinned to the floor and raced through the tune at maximum volume in an imperious style.

Coming on deck one morning a few days out of New York Harbor, we were surprised to see that we were surrounded by other ships. We found ourselves in formation in a convoy. According to the crewmen, this was the largest convoy yet to begin its journey across the North Atlantic. There were ships everywhere: to our left, to our right, behind us and stretched out to the horizon in front of us. There were ships of every size and shape: large vessels such as ours, with cargo piled on the deck; small, stubby steamers; and ships with the unmistakable silhouettes of oil tankers. Out on the fringe of each flank, we could make out the barely visible outline of the feisty little escort vessels, scudding back and forth with their great speed, fulfilling their protective role. The water surrounding us looked like a wintry forest of masts and booms.

The convoy was formed in a series of columns, each column about one-half mile apart. The ships in the column must have been spaced at about six or seven hundred yards. At precise intervals, the entire convoy would change direction, as it zigzagged its way across the Atlantic, as though at the command of some master choreographer.

The crewmembers were very efficient and business-like. But when they occasionally paused at the rail, taking a break for a smoke, they were immediately besieged by all sorts of questions. During the course of the interrogation, we found out that the Sea-Train Texas was a 19,000-ton vessel that had served in the prewar days carrying rolling stock between the mainland and Cuba. However, with great pride and possibly some exaggeration, they told us how their vessel had a single-handedly saved the battle of North Africa, after having delivered a shipload of tanks in time to stop Rommel on his drive toward Alexandria, Egypt.

There were times when, with almost terminal boredom, we would deliberately get lost in the many passageways and make our way into the depths of the ship. On a lower deck we found trucks jammed together, bumper to bumper, in what looked like a truck parking lot. But below that deck was the secret of the ship's name. There, the hold was filled with locomotives and boxcars. The boxcars were unusually small, each with those strange-looking cylindrical bumpers on either end of the car, and all of them wearing their olive drab uniform, ready for the wartime European railway system.

Our reconnaissance was interrupted by the distant sound of exploding depth charges, reminding us that those escort vessels were dead serious in the performance of their duties. Although the submarine threat had diminished by spring of 1944, it was still present and active. It was a sobering interruption. As our days at sea went by, a few men emerged very visibly: these were the profoundly seasick. One man, an acquaintance from West Virginia, became ill on the ferry traveling to Brooklyn. Several others very rapidly joined the ranks of the chronically seasick, a most pathetic group of souls. Sadly, some who had been spending their days in their bunks to accommodate their conditions, made some tragic timing miscalculation, and in doing so, splattered, unforgivably, some of their bunkmates, along with their equipment. Having thus so inexcusably transgressed, they were almost forcibly banished from the sleeping quarters during the daylight hours.

The next logical habitat for them would be the day room. But, alas, there was the abominable piano with its merciless assailant, in itself enough to disquiet an unstable digestive tract, but which, in concert with the ever present smell of food in constant preparation, made that place anathema to the seasick.

This left that small, motley band of sufferers only one recourse – to head for the deck, the most inhospitable place of all, where the pitching and rolling of the vessel was accentuated by the sight and sound of the fury of the waves, and only added to the grief of those suffering from motion sickness. In addition, these men, being on deck, were compelled to wear life jackets, those unique pieces of equipment that had the ability to absorb, greedily, every shipboard odor, especially diesel oil and salt. And then they had to bear the knowledge that those vests had been worn on previous voyages by men in varying stages of seasickness. Those vests clung around the neck like the classical albatross with its "olfactory horror."

Those men then scattered among the landing craft for shelter from the wind and spray, carefully locating themselves within easy commuting distance of the rail. But again, there was the bold smell of fresh paint and the Cosmoline of the tracked landing craft, and located here and there among the landing craft were the ship's ventilators, some of them wafting the warm, stale, and fetid air that was exhaled from below deck, and across those poor victims. It must have seemed to them that everything was conspiring against them to turn the voyage into one great marathon of misery.

When the rest of us would come up on deck, we knew that although out of sight, those poor souls were lurking somewhere. Some of us would sit in the shelter of a landing craft to read, hoping to catch a few rays of warm sunlight; others would stand by the rail watching the waves, lost in their own thoughts. Inevitably, there would be a sudden rush as one of the men would come squirting from between the chains and the landing craft, lunge for the rail, and, hunched over it, vent his peace offering to the gods of the angry waves, retching and heaving in agonizing convulsions.

Without question, most of those men's stomachs must have been purged with the horrid refrain of "Shoo Shoo Baby" echoing around inside their tortured minds. After spending themselves completely, they would disengage themselves from the rail and return, teary-eyed and exhausted, to their lairs to regroup and regain strength for their next assault.

The waters of the North Atlantic in early spring were rough, but little did we foresee the awful potential of their force until we entered a period of storm. As the intensity of the waves began to mount, the ship that had ridden so proudly and comfortable in its element now lost some of that pride and lordly comfort as the fierceness of the storm reduced it to a veritable toy. It would labor to the crest of one huge wave, seem to teeter there for a moment, and then race down into a vast trough with angry claws of water overreaching the bow as though to pull it under, until we were surrounded on all sides by walls of water with but some masts of adjoining ships visible to us.

The next moment an awesome swelling force would heave the vessel to the crest of another mountainous wave, nearly expelling the ship from the water. From our vantage point on the wave's crest, we could briefly see the other vessels battling their way through the boiling cauldron. This tedious and frightening contest kept on relentlessly, hour after hour. One could not help but admire the indomitable courage and skill of those who performed their duties and kept the ship in their respective columns. The inexperienced would simply marvel at how the convoys could possibly find a path to our destination through such a maelstrom of watery rage.

There is an awesome and mystical fascination about the ocean that must turn every man into a philosopher. The myriad questions that flood the mind, quickly brought me to Job's reverential posture of awe in the face of such Divine omnipotence and sovereignty, and caused me to echo the Psalmist's profound question: "What is man that Thou art mindful of him?"

It was a pleasant day, the morning that we walked on deck and discovered that we were in the congenial waters of the Irish Sea. The mood on board began to change rapidly from a stoic forbearance to a more cheerful attitude now that the prospect of docking was closer at hand. Early the next morning, as we awakened, there was an eerie stillness that took us a few moments to comprehend. The engines had stopped – we were in port.

Rushing up on deck and into a cold, damp, penetrating fog, we looked down on a pier with a number of men milling around, waiting. Some of the men on deck started throwing packs of cigarettes, candy, and other articles from our Red Cross packets, down to the men. Someone in our group shouted down to the men, "Where are we?" The answer we got was a puzzling "Cowdif Wiles." We looked at each other with astonishment until the more erudite among us announced, "He said, 'Cardiff, Wales,' you dummies!" Seeing these grown men scamper around the dock after the items thrown to them, we could only guess at the severe shortages they must have experienced. Shortages, no doubt, that must also have given them an affected speech as well.

The unreal world of shipboard life was now over. Now it was back to our quarters to remake our backpacks, gather our duffle bags, and then make our way down the gangplank to the pier. Standing once again in formation beside the vessel that brought us to Europe, a strange reality was creeping up on me in increments. Things that I had perceived only happened to other people were happening to me.

From Cardiff to Normandy

In the cold dampness of April 19, 1944, we disembarked from the large cargo vessel, the Sea-Train Texas, moored in the harbor of Cardiff, Wales.

After the interminable milling around and being issued the mandatory traveling menu of Spam and marmalade sandwiches, we were marched to a nearby train station. This train would introduce us to the European railway coach system, the compartmentalized railway coach, something to which we were completely unaccustomed in the States.

After several hours of travel through the beautiful countryside of southwest England, we arrived in the village of Chard. We marched through the village and were all very impressed with the red tiled roofs that shelter almost every house.

We continued through the village to the outskirts where, on a hill, we could see the nomenclature of a military establishment. There were a series of Quonset huts, but there was also a very sobering sight, a machine gun located in the center of the camp surrounded by slit trenches. This reminded us of the serious fact that the British had faced the real possibility of a German invasion.

British Austerity

Upon entering the Quonset huts we were met with the musty smell that came from the mattress covers stuffed with straw that would be our bedding. There was also the cone shaped stove sitting in a sand box that gave a stinging, eye-burning sensation that we were familiar with, since we had the same type stove and soft coal in our huts in Florida.

We were now coming face to face with the cruel fact that the British had been at war for five long years and the austerity under which they lived was becoming very apparent. This became painfully clear at our first meal in the dimly lit mess hall. The food was not at all what we were accustomed to. We were very forcefully informed that absolutely no edible food would be thrown away, in fact there were guards placed at the garbage cans to assure this. You ate what you were served, period.

It is always amazing how quickly some people come to the forefront. There was a man by the name of Glenn French who quickly boasted that he was related to Bing Crosby. Of course this immediately gave him an elevated stature, which, no doubt was the purpose of revealing this information.

I had always been fascinated with history and I was taken with a sense of awe that I was actually in England. Here was this non-descript eighteen year old from a non-descript small town in Pennsylvania, where six months earlier this possibility never crossed my mind, although I would have eagerly sought such an adventure of actually being in England.

In Basic Training, in the pine and sand of the remote area of Florida, I began to acquire an almost visceral fear and hatred of serving and fighting in the Pacific. That is why at Camp Meade in Maryland, when we were issued our olive drab uniforms, instead of the khaki issue, I experienced a great sense of relief, even an eager excitement, that we were certain to head for the European theatre. Being in England was the fulfillment of that hope and desire.

The double-decker wooden bunks with mattress covers stuffed with stale, lumpy straw were part of the initiation to the reality that we were no longer in that rich, luxurious environment of the United States. I don't remember the name of that camp in Chard, but I would call it Camp Austerity, since that is where I learned the meaning of the word. My admiration of the British people grew considerably.

Our time at that camp was taken up with road marches and endless hours of calisthenics. Since Chard was a very rural village, farm animals seemed to have been given great deference. The roads were used by the farmers to get their cattle to the pastures and because of that the roads were freely spattered with manure. It was tough to retain a straight column and at the same time, avoid the cattle excrement that so carelessly littered our route of march. All of that brought great hilarity among the ranks. It was like marching through a mine field.

I had my own private misadventures in that camp. I was delighted when I came across a rather recent issue of Time magazine. When I left the poorly stocked PX with my precious magazine, I immediately buried my nose in it, oblivious to everything around me. What a shock when I found myself lying in the bottom of one of those slit trenches. Utterly humiliated, I crawled out of that hole, stuck my nose back into the magazine acting as though nothing had happened, when, low and behold there was the second slit trench slyly waiting for this unsuspecting reader. To this day, I don't know whether someone witnessed those spectacular theatrics; I am praying no one did.

It was in the camp in Chard where we were introduced to the befuddling British currency. It took a while for these poor benighted Colonial's to realize that this was real money and not something left over from a game of Monopoly. It took a while to get the farthing, the hapenny, the thrupence, and the full assortment of coinage memorized, but there was a great sense of satisfaction when this was finally accomplished.

Camp Stapley and the Infamous Phrase

Our stay in Chard was very brief when one day we were ordered to gather our gear and mount up on the ubiquitous 6x6, the GI limousine. We passed by the town of Taunton and found ourselves in Camp Stapley. Again, our setting was very rural and very hilly, again surrounded with much cattle fencing and herds of cattle.

This time we were settled in six-man tents, with nothing but cold, damp grass for the floor. Again, road marches and calisthenics occupied much of our time. There were also some "night problems." During the breaks we would lie on our backs and watch German planes being tracked through the night skies. First, one searchlight would capture the gleaming object and skew it on its beam of light, then other searchlights would join in until there was an entire phalanx of beams transfixing the intruder. That group would pass it along to the next series of batteries until it was transferred out of sight. It was remarkable to watch.

We were still dealing with the matter of the austere conditions to which we were completely unaccustomed. We thought that we were being starved to death, since we were still used to the abundance of the meal table in the States.

Camp Stapley had a mess hall that could not serve the entire camp at one sitting and since there were two companies to feed, this created a huge problem. It was finally decided to alternate the feeding of the companies. One day, our company would eat first, then the other company. This worked well, until the first Sunday when the other company decided that the procedure was only in effect on week days. This day, it was our turn to eat first, but there was the other company bullying its way into the mess hall ahead of us. This transgression could not be tolerated. Meal time was becoming like a religious experience. Food was like a sacrament.

The two companies would converge on the mess hall in the form of a V. When the transgressors began forcing their way into the mess hall, there was a huge outcry from our ranks. Things became very nasty and some men almost came to blows. The vitriolic name calling escalated. Opposite me, in the opposing ranks, there was a particularly obnoxious, foul mouthed GI, who seemed to be the cheer leader for the other side. It was always my nature to keep out of melees such as we were involved in, but for some reason, I could no longer restrain myself. In one of my poorer moments, I blurted out that stupid, inane phrase that was so common and considered to be the end-all to any argument. I shouted to my antagonist, "Blow it out your ass!"

Unfortunately, two things converged simultaneously and happened to be my undoing. First; at that exact moment there was a great lull in the shouting, whereby my foolish epithet hung in the air like the Goodyear blimp. Secondly; at the very same moment I shouted that stupid phrase, Sergeant Smedley happened to step between me and the object of my scorn. For some reason, although Sergeant Smedley was championing our company's cause, he thought my vulgarity was directed at him. Needless to say, the good Sergeant took strong umbrage at my indiscretion and came stalking over to me, demanding my name. Despite my feeble protests of innocence, he ordered me to report to the First Sergeant immediately after breakfast. I don't know when I enjoyed a breakfast less than I did that morning.

Smedley's Revenge Backfires

When I left the mess hall, I headed for the First Sergeant's hut. To wake up a First Sergeant on a Sunday morning can be extremely hazardous. When I reported to him, his head remained buried in the pillow and without looking at me, ordered me to report to the Supply Hut and acquire a pick and shovel and report to another Sergeant who had evidently been apprised of my transgression. He was waiting for me and ordered me to dig one of those infamous 6x6x6 holes.

A hole, six feet long, six feet wide and six feet deep and then cover it up. No doubt, there would be a constant parade of wiseacres honing their wits on this poor malefactor, this sorry drudge. Happily, after about three feet of digging and a cascade of insulting witticisms I fortuitously hit a water line. The Sergeant immediately panicked and ordered me to cover up the wretched hole. For that humiliation, Sergeant Smedley would not soon be forgotten or forgiven.

There was one incident at Camp Stapley that was very memorable to me. One noon, after returning from the mess hall, I was alone in the tent. It was Mother's Day. I was overwhelmed with a great feeling of homesickness, and reflecting on the poor son I had been and the grief I must have brought to the heart of my Mother, I broke down and wept. It would be the only time in my almost two years overseas that I experienced such intense homesickness.

The Mapstone Family, The Oasis

Ruins of Glastonbury Cathedral – this is the view I had from my tent at the Abbey camp

Myself with Mrs. Gladys Mapstone

Our stay at Camp Stapley would also be an abbreviated one and the convoy of 6x6's would soon have us on our way to our next camp. We could hardly believe our eyes when we entered the town of Glastonbury and that our camp was within the town. The camp was Abbey Park Camp. It was on the very grounds of the historically famous Glastonbury Cathedral. With my love for history, this was a God-send. At the first opportunity, I took a tour of the Abbey grounds and was so moved by my first real encounter with antiquity.

On occasion, when for some reason, we may have been restricted to camp, I enjoyed sitting in the door of my tent and sketching the ruins. What a memorable picture it was to see those venerable ruins in the month of May, framed by the delicate beauty of the pink blossoms of the apple orchard that separated our camp from the cathedral ruins.

The training at Abbey Camp was much more rigorous. Calisthenics were still an important part of our schedule, but now there was added another element. Several miles outside of the town, there was a brick yard and on the grounds there was one of the most imaginative obstacle courses we had ever run. We took to it immediately. It was always challenging to see who could get through it first. Running it became a very competitive sport. But it was still the forced road marches that were the most demanding. We also had to check out our gas masks in a small concrete building made specifically for that purpose.

Sports were also an important part of our daily schedule. Softball and volleyball were enthusiastically engaged. But in those spare moments, during breaks, the conversation would return to the same subject, the Second Front. That is what the cross Channel invasion of the Continent was referred to, not D-Day, that came after the invasion occurred.

There was a theatre in the center of town that also served as the Town Hall. One evening, I was standing in line, waiting for the theatre to open and there was a young man in front of me, wearing a uniform. We engaged in conversation, particularly, he saw me struggle with the currency. He offered his help and we continued our conversation and sat together through the movie. Upon parting, he offered to meet me the next evening, which I eagerly agreed to.

The following evening when we met, he immediately invited me to his home. His name was David Mapstone. The Mapstone family lived on a farm at the edge of Glastonbury. It was called Northload Bridge Farm. That began a very enduring friendship. It was such a joy to visit with the family. The parents were Horace and Gladys Mapstone. There was an older sister with Down's Syndrome and a younger brother, Geoffrey, a very quiet, but bright young lad. It was with David that I had my first encounter with an English bike. It was almost my undoing, never having driven a bike with hand brakes. The Mapstone's also had two horses and David and I spent happy hours riding through the lovely countryside of Somerset. It was also my great delight to visit the PX and purchase things for the Mapstone family, especially American cigarettes for Mr. Mapstone. They in turn would permit me to enjoy an evening meal with the family. What an honor that was and it was there, again, that I came face to face with the austerity, which to them was a way of life. It was such a pleasure to be away from the Spartan military life that we lived, which was camp life.

Sitting in the Mapstone kitchen was such a warm experience, just listening to the soft, clear accents of the British tongue. Having lived and been raised in a Pennsylvania German area with all of the harsher tones, the quiet conversation in that kitchen was altogether heart-warming.

One evening, Mr. Mapstone entered the kitchen with some alarm. He said that there were rumors that many American bodies had been washed up on the shores of Cornwall. It would be decades later that we would learn of one of the best kept secrets of the war. There was a practice landing operation in process, when German E-boats encountered the unescorted landing craft and attacked at night with catastrophic results. It would also be years later when I would find out that one of the casualties of that disaster was the husband of my wife's closest friend. The irony!

The Cheddar Excursion

One Sunday, we were alerted that there would be a trip to a place called Cheddar Gorge. A convoy of trucks left and the trip was not too long. We indeed, entered a gorge. There were sheer walls of rock and the road wound between them to a small settlement with businesses crowding both sides of the street.

One of the first things mentioned was that there were caverns there where were found the first evidence of pre-historic man in England. It was fascinating, and I purchased two small vases as keep-sakes. We then heard that there was a place serving strawberries and cream. The place was soon filled and what a treat that was. Later, as I wandered among the shops, I overheard someone say that Cheddar Gorge was the place where Augustus Toplady was when inspired to write the words to the hymn, Rock of Ages. That really moved me, and I took a stroll up the winding roadway by myself and just contemplated what he saw that gave birth to those words.

The story was that he was caught in a heavy rainstorm and took shelter in a cleft in the massive rock face. That shelter reminded him of the safety that is found in Christ, and those massive rocks were likened to how substantial and secure those rocks are as found in Christ, who Himself, is the Rock, and our Eternal Shelter.

D-Day, The Great Moment

Then came June 6, 1944: The excitement was monumental! There was one strong element of disappointment, however. We wondered how they could have invaded the Continent without us. Our circumstances where never really explained to us. In our ranks there were men from a number of different branches of the Army. There were Artillery men, Cavalry, of course Infantry and also tankers for Armored units. That explained why there could be such little tactical training. We were too varied. Nevertheless, we were still offended that we were not part of the invasion. Little did we know!!!

Of course, as soon as the invasion was announced, we were immediately restricted to the company area, and it wasn't long before we were all packed and on 6x6's heading for the South of England, Southampton to be precise. Of course we were fortified with the usual menu of Spam and marmalade sandwiches.

During this time, there was an interesting phenomenon that I observed: At the time, Infantry was considered the lowest form of life. We in the Infantry were easily recognized by the blue braid on our overseas caps. Many, who were in the Infantry would secure caps with other braid so as not to have to admit being among the blue braided lepers. It was remarkable, that after the invasion, suddenly the blue braid was much sought after, even by those in other branches.

On the docks of Southampton we were herded aboard a vessel that happened to be under the British flag. When we were ushered below deck to these vast compartments, there were no beds. Finally, we were shown a stack of hammocks and everyone groaned. The problem was that it was difficult to stretch them out fully, which would mean that we would be suspended like a horse shoe. And after surviving the night when breakfast time came, whether it was fact or some demented person in uniform, told us that our breakfast would consist of kidney stew and tea. Of course the crossing was rather rough and soon many of the men parted company with their kidney stew and tea.

Omaha Beach

Last surviving "Mulberry" at Omaha Beach in 1977

Myself with Rosemary Chilcott. Along with Col. Michael Chilcott they own the Old Norman Manor, our hosts during Normandy visit

When, in the morning, we were freed to come up on the main deck, we could scarcely believe our eyes. There, stretched before us was the coast of France, Omaha Beach. There still seemed to be a haze hovering over the entire beach front. Finally, with our full field packs, we were organized on deck in preparation to be received on the landing craft. This would be entirely different than what we expected. The landing craft were raised to the level of the main deck. We would then stand on the railing of the vessel and jump down into the craft from there. The only difficulty was that the water was quite rough and with the swaying of the ship, the landing craft would swing away, five or six feet, and then come crashing back against the side of the vessel. It was a perilous moment, to time your jump at the precise moment that the landing craft struck the vessel, especially being weighed down with all of our equipment.

When the landing craft had its full complement of men, it was lowered into the water. We could only feel for those men who made the initial landing under the full force of enemy fire in waters that were probably more treacherous then what we faced.

By this time, the Mulberry's had been put into place. Those were the docks that had been floated across the Channel and put into place to receive the men and thousands of tons of supplies needed to reinforce the troops already engaged. It was another one of those great moments in my young life, a spine chilling moment to realize that I was standing on French soil.

Not What We Expected

As we made our way up the draw to the high ground, the sound of artillery fire was a very sobering sound. For some reason, a halt was called and we were told that we would be spending the night in place on the high ground overlooking the beach. The activity on the beach and leaving the beach was breathtaking. There was an unending stream of tanks and half-tracks making their way up from the beach and heading inland. Little did I realize that those vehicles belonged to the Division that I would be joining shortly, the 3rd Armored Division.

The next morning, we were moved inland, and came to a large field, surrounded by the infamous hedgerows. We were ordered to set up our tents on the perimeter of the fields, under the cover of the trees that lined the hedgerows.

My first encounter with French civilians was not very uplifting. There was a circle of six or eight men and women having a conversation. One of the men had to urinate. He simply turned around and urinated, never leaving the circle and continued the conversation talking over his shoulder.

There was not much that we could do except go over our weapons, clean them and oil them, but there is only so much of that to be done. This boredom was broken when a rather stubby Colonel came into our field and gathered us around him. He was with the 29th Division and very proudly told us that it was his men who had taken the fields where we bivouacked. We were really awe struck to see what we believed was a real live hero.

Very soon, we were all gathered together and loaded on 6x6's and taken some distance to fields where supplies were stacked. Just acres upon acres of supplies. We were told that we would be unloading the DUK's as they brought loads of all manner of supplies from the beach. This was wearying, but at least we were doing something. But then the rains came. And oh, how it rained.

The fields became a quagmire, what with the vehicles churning up wheel-deep mud. But the work continued. When our work day ended and we were returned to the bivouac area, we stood there with the pockets of our raincoats still full of water and surveyed a rather dismal scene. Everything in our pup tents was soaked. Our blankets were nothing but a soggy mess and this did not bode well for a restful night. In addition to that, our tents and blankets had been invaded by a company of snails. Shaking them out of our blankets and removing them from our duffel bags and whatever was stored in the pup tents, occupied us for some wearying hours.

This was nothing compared to what our comrades engaged in combat with the enemy must have been going through. We could just imagine the horror of living in some muddied pit while under enemy fire, and no possible way to dry out. In a short time, we would join them in that misery.

We must have been involved with the unloading duty for at least three days. Mud splattered, soaked and very weary, but we felt that we were doing a worthwhile duty, so we kept our grumbling to a minimum. As could have been expected, some of the supplies that we handled were food rations and there were a few unfortunate "accidents" where some of the boxes fell, or were somehow damaged and of course that grieved us in that we had to eat the food so it would not go to waste.

Finally, A Home!

One Sunday morning, a jeep drove up to the center of the field, a whistle blew and we were ordered to assemble around the vehicle. An officer stood up with a clip board in his hand, and when we were all gathered, he read off four names. Much to my shock and amazement, my name was among them, considering that there were at least two hundred men in the assembly. We were ordered to quickly gather our gear and return to the jeep.

Very quickly, the four of us returned to the vehicle and we were piled in, clinging to whatever was stable. Since the beachhead was not that deep, it didn't take long to get to our destination. For the second time we passed through the rubble that once was the village of Isigny. We arrived at an area filled with vehicles all garbed in camouflage nets. There were mostly tanks and half-tracks. After we spilled out of the vehicle dragging our gear with us, we were taken to a tent and very shortly an officer emerged. It was Captain Leland Cook, commander of 'D' Co. He was a very impressive man and was no nonsense. He told of the good men that we were replacing and told us that he expected the very best from us.

From there I was taken to men who were bivouacked around a half-track. I was introduced to a Sergeant Bill Adcock, squad leader of the 3rd Rifle Squad, 2nd Platoon of Company 'D'. It was very sobering when I was told that I was replacing a man by the name of John Bateman. He was killed in the first action of the Division. I was assigned to share a pup tent with a man by the name of Fred Hisler from Moline, Ill. Since I was among the first replacements, I was quite wary as to how I would be received, but, fortunately, they accepted me very warmly.

I was now a member of the 36th Armored Infantry Regiment of the 3rd Armored Division. It was a wonderful feeling, finally to have a home after floundering around in the Replacement Pool.

The new men were soon called down to the Company HQ, where

we were given the auspicious responsibility of digging a company latrine. This was no hardship at all. All that mattered was that now I had a home. The squad half-track was D-23 – meaning 'D' Co., 2nd Platoon, 3rd Rifle Squad.

The next morning, we were alerted that there would be religious services held at a certain time. We were informed as to where each Chaplain would be located. Since I was Protestant, I went to the appropriate corner where the Protestant Chaplain would meet with us. This was an ominous foreboding since religious services during the week usually preceded battle. I shall never forget the text that was used; He spoke from the Book of Luke 5:36-39. It dealt with putting new wine into old wine skins. I am still baffled as to the pertinence of that Scripture, although, I am sure, it was well meaning.

Later in the day, we moved out and fell into line with a convoy of half-tracks. It was during the time of travel that I began to learn more about the men and their first combat action. They spoke about a railroad gun firing from a tunnel near St. Lo. How accurate this was, I don't know. But it was that alleged railroad gun that cost John Bateman his life.

The Baptism ... Combat

As darkness came, things became more and more tense since the volume and nearness of artillery fire indicated that the forward lines were not too distant. At times such as that, on that slender beachhead, the congestion was terrible and movement was at a snail's pace. We finally entered some fields, and tanks and half-tracks began coiling around the perimeter of the fields. Everything came to a halt and we dismounted our half-tracks and I was partnered with an older man. His name was Pop Waters. Suddenly firing began all around us and we hit the ground. I found myself lying on the ground by a hedge that bordered a roadway. Men were running along the roadway and I quickly realized that they were German soldiers. It was then that some of the tanks opened fire adding to the confusion of the rifle and machine gun fire. Then as quickly as it all started, it was over.

Much to our chagrin, we later found out that someone had moved us into the wrong position; in fact, they had moved us into a German position. Pop Waters and I then set about digging our foxhole. The rest of the night was rather quiet, as Pop and I took turns standing guard. I must admit, that after it was over, there was a great sense of calm within me.

Pop Waters had acquired the reputation of being quite eccentric. He was not too favorably disposed to military discipline. He was not a big man, and his age of the mid-thirties, with a balding head and a rim of reddish hair, made him very unique. That night was the first time that I met him and he was the squad BAR man. By the time, after being wounded, I rejoined the company in the beginning of September, Pop Waters was the Platoon Sergeant. By then, he had established himself as one of the foremost combat leaders in our company. He had combat sense that few men possess, a sense that seemed to be native to this backwoods farmer from the Mid-West.

Next morning, as the sun rose, we could see some of the results from that brief, confused action of the night before. There was a German tank on a sloping hill, with a crewman of the tank draped over the barrel of the cannon. An unforgettable sight. Seeing the setting we were in by daylight made me marvel that with all the firing in that brief span of time there were not more casualties. The tanks and infantry formed up in a field that was nearby a yellow stucco structure – what appeared to be a church building. We began moving forward, with the tanks firing into the hedgerows as we approached them. There was a tank with a bulldozer blade and after some time, that tank pushed an opening through the hedgerow and then pulled back. Two or three other tanks then proceeded through the opening and fanned out in the next field. This was a slow, tedious process, but the only sensible way to make any progress.

The Face of Death

The Germans seemed to be masters at utilizing every terrain feature to their advantage, and the hedgerows were prime means of stopping our advance with their skillfully deployed machine guns, covered by very accurately used mortars. We infantry would take shelter behind the tanks to escape the machine gun fire, but the mortar rounds were not easily defended against in the open fields. Their anti-tank guns took a horrible toll of the tanks.

We progressed very cautiously and very slowly, field by field. We came to one opening into a rather narrow field and this time, there were no tanks with us in that field. We could see that directly opposite there was a gateway to the next field. I was with a man by the name of John Kollenberg. We decided to make a dash across the open field to the next hedgerow. The grass was about knee high and we were taking fire. About midway across the field, we saw directly ahead of us, at the base of the next hedgerow, a German soldier trying to get to his feet. Since there were two of us, and he was alone, I was sure that we had a prisoner. But, in a split second, John fired off several rounds, striking the man.

I was determined on one thing, and that was to get out of the line of fire and to the shelter of that next hedgerow. The German soldier that John had struck was directly ahead of me and I had no choice but to hit the ground right next to him. Here, next to me, was this German soldier. What a terrible moment. He was moaning quietly and I was sure that he was dying. I was completely mesmerized with my first encounter with battlefield death. Lying just a few feet from me, I could see the color slowly drain from his face. He was gone. Here was a real German soldier, in three dimensions, right next to me. It troubled me that the man was not taken prisoner. Those are the split second decisions that are made on the battlefield that have horrible consequences.

It was a plodding method of fighting, one field at a time and with the constant storm of machine gun fire and the deadly accuracy of

German mortars. It seemed that they withheld the bulk of their artillery fire until the end of the day when the day's drive came to a halt. Then, watch out, because it came with fury.

It was at the end of one such day that we had caught a particularly fierce artillery barrage. After it lifted, I went to the next hedgerow that was at the highest point of the ground we had captured. I looked over the top and my heart sank when I looked into the distance and saw, seemingly, hundreds of more hedgerowed fields just like the several we had taken that one day. I thought to myself that we'll never get out of this mess, especially when we could see our casualties mounting and for such little real estate.

The Moment of Truth

In Normandy, in July, our tank and infantry unit had been brought under extremely heavy machine gun fire in a hedged field resplendent with brilliantly colored poppies. As I lay in the grass beside a tank, hugging the earth under fierce, grazing fire, I could see, near me, flowers snipped from their stems or exploding in a shower of petals. The scene was a vivid portrait of the bitter anomalies of war; Sherman tanks squatting in the midst of poppies and angry bursts of machine gun fire slashing through the flowering shrubs that graced the hedgerows that surrounded us.

We finally broke out onto a narrow lane and moved slowly forward for some distance. There was a 6 or 8-foot embankment with heavy foliage on the left side of the lane, and on the right was a 3-foot stone wall that separated the lane from an open field. It was barely wide enough for a Sherman tank. Trees lined both sides of the lane and overarching it, turning it into nothing but a green tunnel. There were at least five tanks in the column and the infantry was single file, between the row of tanks and the stone wall. Our 3rd Rifle Squad was in the lead and I happened to be near the head of the column with our Platoon Leader, Lt. Shedd.

After moving slowly for some distance, the column of tanks and Infantry came to a halt. Then there was a conversation between our platoon leader, Lt. Shedd, and the lead tank commander. The tank commander said that he would not move his column of tanks until the intersection had been cleared. Approximately seventy-five yards ahead, an intersection could be seen where a similarly narrow lane bisected the one upon which we were advancing and there was a small brick structure located on the right of the intersection. After the conversation ended, Lt. Shedd ordered me, since I was near him, to advance to the intersection and check for any enemy vehicles or guns that might be there. I made my way forward on the right side of the roadway, hugging the wall and in a low crouch cautiously moved toward the road junction. When I reached the small brick building at the intersection, I checked carefully in all three directions, and saw nothing of a threatening nature, neither gun nor vehicle.

I made my way back to the head of the column and reported to Lt. Shedd that I had seen nothing of either enemy vehicles or guns. When I made my report, I was standing to the right front of the lead tank. Then, either by coincidence or by design, a heavy outburst of machine gun fire from the right front across the field raked the column. Everybody's attention was immediately focused on that area to try to pick up the position of the offending gun. At that instant, out of the corner of my eye, I saw a flash and a cloud of dust only a few yards beyond the intersection where I had been just a few minutes previously, and instantly, the tank beside me was hit. There must have been a Panzerfaust team concealed in the heavy foliage, dug into the embankment just beyond the intersection. In the moment of diversion, it fired that deadly blast. The explosion of that round against the tank caught me like a wallop.

The blast was so powerful that it felt as though someone had slammed me across the front of my body with a 2x4. I knew that I was hit because my neck and chin were bloody and burnt, and my field jacket was almost shredded.

As I made my way toward the back of the unit, I passed men crouched against the stone wall. I received words of encouragement and comfort as I passed by them. "Tough luck, kid!" "You'll be OK!" "Everything will be alright kid!" I went back some distance and then lay down in a ditch where a medic came and gave me first aid and a shot of morphine. In a very short time, I was joined by two badly burned tankers who had somehow managed to extricate themselves from the burning tank.
One of the great dreads that I had was how I might respond when I might be hit. When I saw some men, who were not that seriously wounded, carry on and cry and curse, I feared that I might respond the same way. I did not want to disgrace myself, my family or my God with such conduct. Instead, there was a great sense of peace as I lay there in that ditch.

Another self-imposed myth that I had been living with was that I was convinced that my role would always be that of a spectator; that others would be down on the playing field, while I would occupy the bleachers. That myth died in that ditch when the fact hit me, "It happened to me".

The Improbable Had Happened

Normandy medical unit

Field hospital in Normandy

Because of the congestion in the narrow lane, it took a while
before they were able to bring up a medical half-track. It didn't
take very long before we arrived at a large tent in a pasture with a
huge Red Cross emblazoned in several places. There was nothing
but a grass floor. Quickly, I was x-rayed and, just as quickly, I
found myself on an operating table with a huge greenish light
overhead.

The nurse then began applying the anesthesia and said to me,
"Now tell me all about what happened." Evidently speaking would
hasten the affect of the anesthetic. I began mumbling something,
but the effect of the anesthetic was so pleasant that it was like the
happy hour. It seemed as though I was lying on some soft velvety
whirl pool and I was gently drawn down into unconsciousness.

Later, when I awakened and became lucid enough to investigate my injuries, I found that my neck and chin had been burned by the heat of that penetrating missile, and there were other bandages on the upper and lower part of my body, which I surmised, covered shrapnel wounds. Lying on my chest and tied around my neck was a medical packet. I checked the contents and was surprised to find the projectile to a rifle bullet inside.

The Blast and The Slug

Sometime later, the doctor came by and knelt in the grass beside my litter. He asked me some questions as to how I felt and then I said, "Doctor, there must have been a mistake. I was hit by a Panzerfaust, not small arms fire." The doctor replied, "I don't know about that, all I know is I removed that slug from your lower abdomen."

Can you imagine, lying in a hospital bed for days and even weeks and contemplating the great improbability of what had happened: To be hit twice, instantaneously and simultaneously by two different weapons and still be alive. That was the miracle. I had shrapnel and burns to my chin. Supposing the blast had been five inches higher, I could also have been blinded.

Shortly after that, several of us found ourselves lying on our litters on the tarmac of the landing strip above Omaha Beach. There, looming over us was a C-47 Hospital plane.

A Chaplain moved among us, kneeling down beside us and praying over us. How appropriate to be dismissed from that awful Beachhead with the words of God's Grace ringing in our ears.

The Normandy Ward

The U. S. Army Hospital, Plant 4178, was pleasantly situated in the beautiful countryside of southwest England. The newly finished hospital had been empty, waiting for the first flood of casualties that would pour across the English Channel after our forces had landed somewhere on the Continent of Europe.

But now D-Day had come and gone, and the Allied Armies had landed on the beaches of Normandy. In the weeks that followed, Army ambulances would make their endless circuits between the docks of south England and the hospital to unload their mutilated cargo. As soon as the airstrip was completed on top of Omaha Beach, airfields in south England were added to the collection points for the casualties that were flown to England and brought to the hospital by ambulance. It was by the route of the Omaha Beach airstrip that I found myself in this hospital. I had suffered a gunshot wound of the abdomen and some shrapnel wounds from a Panzerfaust on July 10 in Normandy.

The weeks that I spent in the hospital were a tranquil interlude after the tumultuous preceding weeks of rapid movement and intense action. The large, freshly painted ward was already filled to capacity and was always alive with the banter of unquenchable G.I. humor and ongoing teasing with the nurses. If there seemed to be an air of exaggerated laughter, even among the more seriously wounded, it was simply the outpouring of sheer joy, the exhilaration of just being alive. After all, these men were the survivors of that still perilously clung-to Normandy Beach-head. There were men from the 1st, the 4th, and the 29th Divisions, who had made the assault on Omaha and Utah Beaches. There was a Ranger or two who had participated in taking the German position on the precipitous Point du Hoc. There were glidermen and paratroops from the vaunted 82nd and 101st Airborne Divisions, who had fought in isolation, exploiting enemy weaknesses to gain their vital objectives. There were men from other units, such as the

3rd Armored Division, who joined the battle later, and who had their baptism of fire in the fierce battle of the hedgerows, where every field was transformed into an enemy fortress and the murderous crossfire took an unconscionable toll of lives.

In the bed beside me was a young soldier who still trembled with fear. After being seriously wounded, he had lain in his foxhole beneath the dead body of a fellow soldier for two days. In another bed, close by, was a gliderman with an extremely heavy accent, from the 82nd Airborne. He told us how he had paraded before Mussolini as a young soldier in the Italian Army, until his mother was able to smuggle him out of Italy to the U.S. He told us about his glorious entry into France, how, when his glider hit the ground, it broke up on impact and he was hurled through the air, only to come to a sliding halt with his face buried in the manure of a Norman cow. There was another man across the aisle from me who filled only half his bed. He had been run over by a tank and had his legs amputated below the hips. He stared stoically at the ceiling for hours on end to avoid the painful downward glance at the flat, taut blanket where his legs and feet should have been.

A special bond quickly developed among the men in the ward. Strong friendships were quickly forged. The ambulatory patients would move among those who were bedfast, encouraging them, asking about their units, hoping to find mutual acquaintances within their ranks. They would light cigarettes for those who were helpless and run small, necessary errands.

There were men in all manner of casts, some in body casts, others in leg casts that were elevated in traction, and still others in arm casts, with the arms locked forward of the body in crooked positions, appearing like mimes frozen in mid-performance. There was always a significant change of mood among the men in the ward as night approached. It was a puzzling phenomenon. Was it the fear of the isolation that quiet and darkness bring? Was it the apprehension of each man receding into his own private arena of hell, where in sleep, the subconscious mind would resurrect a thousand different scenarios of torment that he had already endured?

During the night there were frequent periods of unusual quiet when I would suppress sleep and in an almost childlike manner, surrender myself to the marvelous security of the ward. I would try to fasten my mind on enjoying the soft, clean comfort of the hospital bed. Lying in the silence, I would listen to the gentle rhythm of my own breathing, the most elementary and gratifying reminder of being alive. For me, to be awake was the dream; to sleep was the nightmare.

Often my reverie was intruded upon by the audible torment of those who slept. There would be a sudden outburst as someone in a nightmare gave out a pathetic cry for help. Another would curse loudly in a frenzy of helplessness over a weapon that would not fire; someone else screamed orders to a squad that did not exist. To hear, welling out of the darkness, the pleading, plaintive cry of a man calling for a friend who would not answer, was almost heartbreaking.

Meanwhile, up and down the long, darkened ward, deep into the night, there would be sporadic clicks and flashes of cigarette lighters, as trembling hands tried to light unsteady cigarettes held between the quivering lips of men who had become hostages to that felt clutch of sleeplessness. For the sleepless as well as the sleeping fell victim to the torments of the night. Unrepentant darkness, which knows neither truce nor armistice, would relentlessly do its demon work, constantly awakening the fear-laden memories of battlefield terror. Unforgetting, unforgiving darkness, with a sly viciousness, would again and again lacerate those tender, unsutured inner wounds and would not let them heal. And those nights would be the cruel harbinger of decades of similar nights to come, when time and distance would neither diminish nor assuage the unremitting pain.

During the night there was always the sound of nurses on constant patrol, quietly and efficiently moving among the beds with their flashlights, checking on each man. At some beds, there were extended pauses as they whispered consolingly to those who could not sleep. To others, with the same comforting tenderness, they administered medication when the pain was no longer bearable. The flick of the light switch in the morning, accompanied by the cheery voices of the day nurses, signaled the distinct change of the mood that would restore the easy light-heartedness that made the days so different and almost pleasant.

One day the daily routine of the ward was interrupted with a great stir of excitement. A full Colonel and his party had come to the hospital. When the Colonel and his entourage entered our ward, we found out that he had come to present the Purple Heart to each of us. What made this particularly auspicious was that this was the first time the awards had been made in that hospital since the Normandy invasion.

Those of us who were ambulatory were ordered to stand in front of our beds, while the Colonel's Aide read the names and the serial numbers, and then the Colonel made the presentation. What a motley and unmilitary looking group we must have been, standing in front of our beds, dressed in our pajamas, bathrobes and canvas hospital slippers.

When the Colonel, followed by his splendidly attired entourage, took his position in front of me, he paused and looked at me. He then asked, "How old are you, son?" "Eighteen years old Sir," I replied. "What the hell are you doing over here?" he bellowed out across the ward! I replied, "I'm just very proud to be here."

Some weeks later, I underwent another operation. In Normandy, in the field hospital, when the projectile had been removed from my abdomen, the wound was stuffed with Vaseline gauze to ensure proper healing. Now that the wound had healed properly, a second operation was needed to close the wound.

Following the operation, I was placed alone in a room. One day, the door suddenly opened, and several nurses burst into my room singing, "Happy Birthday." One of the nurses had seen on my records that August 7, was my nineteenth birthday, so they had brought me small gifts. Such thoughtfulness and personal concern in the midst of their uniquely busy and demanding schedules was a most moving experience. It showed what a special breed of people they really were.

For my period of rehabilitation, I was transferred to a hospital near Hereford, England. It was there that I received some sad news. During my stay in Glastonbury, Somerset, at Abbey Camp prior to the invasion, I had been befriended by the Mapstone family, a wonderful, solid, English family. The warmth of their home had been a comforting refuge from the austerity of camp life. Having learned of my injury and subsequent hospitalization, this kind family had hired a car at great expense and, in gas-starved England, had traveled many miles to visit me in the hospital. Unfortunately, they had arrived at the hospital the day after I had left to begin my rehabilitation program. It was with a heavy heart that within a short time I began my journey across the Channel without having seen my dear friends. The balancing consolation was that I was eager to rejoin the men of 'D' Co, the 36th Armored Infantry Regiment of the 3rd Armored Division where I belonged.

Scherpenseel

Hastenrath killing field – sixteen American tanks destroyed

With Oliver Wiggs who was in one of the three surviving tanks chased by Hans Zeplien and the Panzerfaust (also see page 185)

The brooding skies of November were busy with swiftly moving clouds that hurried over the hills surrounding the village of Schevenhutte.

Most of our platoon was quartered in a house close by a swimming pool. The pool had been drained and had a layer of wet autumn leaves pasted to its sloping floor. Extending from the house and continuing along most of the one side of the pool was a long roofed porch. Several of us preferred the meager shelter of the porch to the noisy confusion of the house.

On the other side of the pool was a small stream that flowed underneath a bridge and causeway that joined the house to the main roadway. Between the stream and the narrow roadway was an apron of grass where a battery of 155 mm howitzers stood silently. Our half-tracks were parked at prudent intervals, hugging the base of a steep wooded slope that rose sharply from the roadway.

The living room of the house was the focal point for the activities during those several days of waiting. The room had the odd combination of rather fine furniture that was almost smothered beneath the dreary olive drab clutter of clothing and equipment of an Armored Infantry company. Elegant chairs had field jackets and cartridge belts draped over their backs, with empty canteen covers and entrenching tools dangling from them.

A beautiful sofa strained beneath the weight of several men enjoying its momentary and uncommon comfort. Blanket rolls were stuffed between the legs of chairs and tables, ready to be unfurled at night on any spot large enough to accommodate the body of a man.

An upright piano had its top littered with canteens, mess kits, and discarded K-ration boxes, all conspiring to diminish the dignity of the venerable instrument. A small table was almost obscured by a large box of 10 in 1 rations that had been hastily torn open and already half emptied of its contents. And in the corner were stacked several M-1 rifles with a solitary BAR standing awkwardly among them.

Men stood, sat and squatted, filling every inch of space. Some were drinking coffee or hot chocolate; others were munching on food from the easily accessible 10 in 1 ration box. Simultaneously, there were at least half dozen conversations volleying back and forth, each conversation elbowing its way through the crowded noise of the smoke filled room. All of this bedlam was surrounded by four walls covered with gaudy, blue and red wallpaper that made the scene an absurd cacophony of sound and color.

The few of us who preferred the lesser shelter of the roofed porch were at least spared some of the consequences of the overcrowded house. We could prepare a meal without having a mess kit kicked across the floor. We could drink a cup of coffee without some errant elbow splashing the hot beverage into our face. It also meant sleeping without fear of being stomped by a combat boot as some sleepy soldier groped his way to the door to attend to a personal emergency. The quiet roofed porch was also ideal for letter writing. Finally, writing letters with substance instead of those perfunctorily scrawled V-mail letters that said little except that we were still alive.

The letters written and the letters received were that sacred umbilical cord to home and sanity that helped us to maintain our mental and spiritual equilibrium. That time of rest also helped to reaffirm our humanity.

One morning I decided to go to the half-track to retrieve something I needed. As I crossed the bridge, I noticed intense activity around the howitzers. Their muzzles were elevated so sharply that it appeared they were preparing some celestial salute rather then firing on some distant target.

By the time I reached the half-track, which was forward of the battery, one of the guns fired, almost lifting me out of my boots. The thunderous reverberations escalated to a deafening roar as the other guns joined in the bombardment.

The firing of the guns was the signal for us to be alerted to prepare to move out. It didn't take long to gather our few pieces of equipment and mount our half-tracks. The sound of shouts as orders were bellowed out filled the intervals between the battery firings.

Within a short time we were making our way through the rubble filled streets of Schevenhutte and soon emerged from the shelter of the rugged hills where we had been waiting. We were greeted with the sound of an enormous, area-wide artillery barrage. Hundreds of other guns were firing in concert with that lonely battery that had awakened us so rudely by the swimming pool. In the distance could be heard the unmistakable resonant sound of the "Long Toms", other artillery pieces, adding their deep throated voices to the choir of misery already inflicting its deadly damage on the waiting German troops.

Above the low overcast skies we could hear the drone of the engines of the heavy bombers. The area sparkled with the aluminum chaff that had been dropped to confuse the enemy Radar in advance of the "heavies".

In the distance, under the low overcast skies, we could see swarms of medium bombers heading for enemy targets. Darting here and there, sometimes disappearing into the cloud cover were American fighter planes free-lancing their way through the skies looking for enemy planes or targets of opportunity.

The snail-like stop and go movement of the column was always frustrating and maddening. After a while, jesting and other conversation within the half-track began to wear thin. The anticipation, the forebodings and the fears began taking their toll with an uneasy silence descending on the vehicle.

The column finally eased off the roadway and into a large open field, apparently a sugar beet field. The half-tracks began coiling, but within seconds, an artillery barrage of unusual ferocity came slamming in all around us.

My position in the half-track was the responsibility of manning the water cooled 30 caliber machine gun mounted on the left rear of the vehicle. Because of my position on the machine gun, I was also responsible for opening the heavy door at the rear of the "track". I was constantly teased about getting the door open quickly in the event of an emergency, since the latch was quite cumbersome.

When the artillery barrage came in, I had the door open in a split second, however, that must not have been fast enough since almost everyone bailed out over the sides of the half-track. However, once we hit the ground and began slogging through the mud, there was really no place to go for cover since it was a large, flat, open field.

The Rewards and Perils of Leadership

In mid-November of 1944 our unit was located in Germany inside the Siegfried Line, in the vicinity of Stolberg. On the 16th of November we were poised along with other units to participate in an offensive to secure some high ground in the Hastenrath-Scherpenseel front. The weather during the preceding weeks had been intolerable, with incessant periods of rain, turning the terrain into a sodden mess. Walking was mostly a series of lurching, sliding and wallowing motions.

When the assault began, we were in immediate reserve and after moving forward some distance, we left the roadway and came to halt in a large field. There was a peculiar smell that hung heavy in the air and turned out to be that of decaying sugar beets mixed with equal parts of the usual scent familiar to the environs of a farm. The trees and bushes that fringed the area were all draped with strips of aluminum foil dropped by our planes in order to confuse enemy radar, giving the appearance of tinsel having been thrown haphazardly onto the boughs of a Christmas tree.

We were ordered to dismount from our half-track and prepare for digging in. Our squad leader led us away two by two to the area that was assigned as our position and ordered us to dig in. I found myself partnered with a new, young soldier who had just joined us. His newness was so conspicuous because of his neat uniform, his brand new equipment, and even the chalk smudge of his embarkation number still on his steel helmet. Before we had taken too many steps through the mire, I became quickly aware that I had a very lively conversationalist for a companion. Most of the conversation, however, took the form of questions.

"Where are you from?"
"Pennsylvania, near Allentown."
"How long have you been with the Company?"
"Since the first days of July."

"How old are you?"

"Nineteen in August."

"Did anything bad ever happen to you, like getting hit or something?"

"Yeah, back in Normandy."

"Did it hurt?"

"It didn't feel good."

No sooner had our squad leader left to assign the next team to its position, then this young soldier blurted out to me in a most apologetic tone that he had never been in combat before, as though that fact had been a deliberate plot on his part, and not having been in combat before, he really didn't know what to do, how to conduct himself, or what was expected of him. Then he made the startling suggestion that since he had never been in combat before and I had, he thought it only fair that he should dig the foxhole. He would gladly do all the digging if I would just tell him what to do. Having someone dig a foxhole for me was a luxury I had never before enjoyed; indeed, having minimal authority of any kind to a nineteen-year-old PFC was as alien as water is to the moon.

As I stood there observing this frightened novice, I began experiencing a strange, but marvelous metamorphosis. I began seeing myself in an altogether different light. With the care and keeping of this solitary mortal creature thrust upon me, I realized that I must now comport myself in an appropriate manner, in view of my new and unfamiliar responsibility.

I told him that one did not simply plunge into the matter of digging a foxhole; there were certain vital matters to be considered. Trying frantically to think of some reasons to justify the remark I had just blundered into, I said, as I strode back and forth, that first the matter of the proximity of trees must be considered because of the deadliness of tree bursts, and then there was the matter of an adequate field of fire and, of course, the displacement of the ground from the hole in order to build a parapet. He said very sheepishly that he never realized that there was so much involved in digging a hole, but I reminded him that he had much to learn.

As this metamorphosis continued, I noticed a decided lowering in the tone of my voice as I spoke to him, and not only was there a lowering in my voice, but I also detected the unusual inflection of command as I instructed him.

Carefully surveying the area with the eye of an engineer, striding back and forth with several studied pauses now and then, I faced him abruptly and told him I had now made my decision. With a masterstroke, I pulled my bayonet from its scabbard and, bending over, I outlined, with its point, the dimension of the foxhole in the soft earth. Then, with dramatic flourish, I jabbed the bayonet into the center of the outline, (This impressed the poor devil no end) and with a voice loaded with as much authority as I could muster, I said, "This is precisely where I want the foxhole dug!"

It then occurred to me, that since I had now undertaken my first combat command, my next important decision was the matter of the proper stance I should take. Should I stand with legs astride and my hands on my hips? No. I thought this too intimidating. I elected instead to assume a more democratic posture. I would simply slouch on the ground beside him and direct operations from there.

As he stood there briefly, I could see he was undergoing an emotional spasm. He then remarked that he had just been struck with the historic significance of the moment. This would be his first combat mission and he was now entering the select ranks of the combat infantry soldier. I agreed that he would never forget this 16th day of November 1944, because it was on this day that he had for the first time unsheathed his entrenching tool in anger.

As I gazed solemnly out into the distance, I said that I too remembered vividly, and with much pain, the similar moment in my own life when I had been initiated into the ranks of this combat unit. I felt it unnecessary, however, to burden him with the unhappy details of that occasion, when back in the battle-ravaged hedgerows of Normandy; I had joined this Company after it had been bloodied in its first action. It was on that day, that, for the first time, I had also unsheathed and brandished my entrenching tool in true anger, when our good Company Commander, Captain Jack Cook, had recommended to me that I dig a hole, a hole of an adequate dimension to accommodate the baser needs of the Company.

My new ward stood silently for another few seconds, savoring his moment in history. Then he threw himself into his new mission with vengeance; his entrenching tool taking angry bites of earth from within the carefully delineated area that I had marked for him. With each shovelful of earth exploding into the air, there seemed to be an accompanying question: "Where are all those tanks and half-tracks loaded with Infantry that were with us when we started? Where are they now and why are we so alone?" "With that large, heavily armored, open half-track that's like a big hole on wheels setting there, why do we have to dig this one?" "Do you think I'll freeze when the first shells start coming in?" "Do German soldiers smell different than we do?" "Is it true that when bullets come real close, they don't whine, but really snap?" "Is it true that some soldiers get so scared that they end up walking with their legs real straight after having soiled their pants?"

Whenever his steel helmet appeared above ground level, another spade full of earth erupted out of the hole, followed immediately by another barrage of questions. It appeared that the matter of fear seemed to have an obsessive hold on him. Did being scared make him a coward? Would being afraid make him do funny things? Wasn't everybody scared when they went into combat for the first time? Very quietly, I explained to him that he should not look at fear as his mortal enemy, but rather, as his friend. I told him that controlled fear would infinitely sharpen all of his senses and that controlled fear would give him strengths he had heretofore never experienced.

I astonished myself with the ease and calmness and matter of factness with which every question was answered. What a delightful and heady feeling! It was then that he paused in his digging and transformed his muddied pit into a confessional booth. Very warmly, he confessed to me how fortunate he felt to have found and buddied up with such a wise and experienced combat mentor; it must have been all this accrued wisdom that had accounted for my having survived so long. I told him that I did not disagree with his very perceptive estimate, and that he would do well to take heed to the counsel of those who were more experienced and wiser and older than he. (It had been determined during the course of the interrogation that I was at least 10 months his senior.) This would certainly enhance his chances for survival; otherwise, he faced a most dismal and uncertain future. With that, he resumed his digging with even more enthusiasm, as he seemed very intent on further impressing his new confidante.

As I sat there totally intoxicated with the rarefied air of my new role, I began hearing mutterings rise from the hole, and along with the mutterings I could hear the ominous sound of the entrenching tool striking some resisting object. These sounds persisted as he struck again and again at the stubborn culprit that had stopped his downward progress. He would pause now and then and give me looks of almost total despair, sensing possibly that his first important mission was about to end in complete failure. He then readjusted his entrenching tool so that it took the form of a pick and again began viciously attacking the obstruction that had brought matters to a stalemate.

Realizing that in leadership there are times when the leader must join the troops in the field, with real irritation, I decided that I must descend from the stratosphere of my lofty new realm to see what the problem was. Visibly showing my annoyance, I ordered the serf to vacate the hole. Confident that in a very short time, as I would bring my experience to bear on the matter, there would be a gasp of awe wafting over my shoulder from my eager observer, as I quickly and efficiently resolved the problem. Getting down on my knees, with my buttocks pointing skyward, I reached down to the bottom of the hole and began vigorously clawing and scraping at the dirt with my hands to determine the nature and magnitude of the alleged, unyielding obstruction. As I scraped and scraped at the dirt, in absolute horror I uncovered a very large and very cylindrical object. Immediately, I suspended all breathing.

With eyes wide and eyeballs locked at rigid attention, lest even their movement detonate what, by now, after the savage blows it had taken, must be a very angry unexploded shell, I arose unsteadily on very shaky legs. In enforced wordlessness, I groped for and grabbed the shoulder of my cohort and led him away on tiptoes. Then that most insidious and demeaning of all instincts, the instinct of self-preservation, treacherously commandeered all my senses and all my energy, and with a bewildered and disenchanted neophyte in tow, I fled in shameless haste from what I was certain was an impending Vesuvius, alas, leaving behind, by that mound of earth, all my bravado, amidst the still steaming wreckage of my skyrocketing career as a military leader.

And as though in final insult, there lay silently on the ground that abominable entrenching tool, pointing mockingly to the carefully selected site of the abandoned foxhole. How fleeting and how transient the glories of leadership!

Back to Business

Fortunately, at the same time, our platoon leader ordered everyone back to the half-tracks. Our vehicle began churning through the muddy field heading for the narrow opening that led onto the roadway. Behind us we left the eerie circles and scrolls in the mud of what had been a large, orderly field of unharvested sugar beets.

As dusk approached, we could see ahead of us the outline of the village of Werth. We approached the village from its northern edge. As we made a right turn down the village street, we passed a Sherman tank on fire, outlined against the horizon, burning briskly and casting a plume of black smoke into the November air.

Werth was situated on the slope of high ground with a panoramic view overlooking a large open field of pasture and sugar beets. The village of Scherpenseel lay to our right front and the town of Hastenrath lay ahead of us at the distant end of the large, open field.

As we proceeded down the street, our half-tracks were positioned at intervals, one at a time, and our platoon was assigned to houses squad by squad. Pop Waters, our platoon Sergeant, had finished placing the squads and was returning from quite a distance down the street, when suddenly, another heavy artillery barrage came crashing into our position. Shells exploded furiously all along the street.

One moment, before us, we saw Pop Waters, then a shell exploded in the road in front of him and there was nothing but smoke and debris. A split second later Pop emerged through the smoke and debris, not having missed a step, wearing his 'tanker suit', his wool knit cap and carrying his "Tommy Gun". Pop had nothing but contempt for the steel helmet and showed an air of disdain as he continued through the maelstrom of steel, determined that nothing should deter him from his appointed duties.

By this time, darkness had fallen and our squad guard roster for the night had already been made up when the automatic and small arms fire erupted. There was a counter-attack under way. We could barely make out some of the shadowy figures coming up through the cemetery that was located in front of our house. The artillery barrage had probably set the stage for this attack. Everyone was pouring fire from the windows as well as from the half-tracks parked in the street below our second floor position. We saw one man go down. He must have been caught by the slugs from the 50 caliber machine gun mounted in the ring mount of the half-track. His body bounced around pathetically like a rag doll.

The attacking force must have been a small one because the effort was soon broken and our position opposite the cemetery was again secure. And as we settled down for our routine of guard duty and sleeping, one new man who had just joined us from the Air Corps, casually asked where his bed was. We all looked at him in wonderment and with quite some amusement. We simply pointed to the floor and told him to pick his spot. It was as simple as that.

Information as to what was going on was usually sparse and found out piecemeal. We did know that Werth had been taken earlier by Colonel Lovelady's men. In the process of the attack, tanks of I Co. of the 33rd Regiment had broken out into the large open field and attacked toward Hastenrath, suffering heavy casualties. The Armored Infantry unit assigned to follow the tanks for some reason, failed to do so. That left the few surviving tanks and their crews isolated near the outer buildings of Scherpenseel and Hastenrath.

It had been rumored during the night that our Company Commander had been ordered to march us through Scherpenseel and then to join the remnant of the attacking force in Hastenrath, which was immediately adjacent to Scherpenseel. It was reported that our C.O. had refused to do so, since there was no knowledge that Scherpenseel had indeed been cleared, which, in fact it was not.

November 17th was a rather dreary, unpleasant day when we left our position in Werth. The Infantry formed up with the tanks and began moving into the attack. There was approximately 500 yards of open ground between the last building in Werth and the first building in Scherpenseel. As soon as the column emerged from the shelter of the buildings of Werth, we were greeted with an unprecedented volume of fire. It seemed to come from all directions; to our right of the roadway was a low ridge that was heavily defended with rifle and automatic weapons and we could hear the muffled sound of mortars behind them.

From our left we could actually see the white hot slugs from guns or tanks throwing direct fire, along with the piercing screams that high velocity guns produced, as they tried to smash our tank force. Incoming artillery shells were sending up spouts of mud and field debris all around us.

Ross Overholt, a good friend of mine, was a few feet behind me in the column. I came to believe that it is true that you don't hear the shell that will get you, because the ground suddenly erupted in an embankment beside us, showering us with cascades of mud. The shell that landed between us was a dud! We just looked at each other with stunned disbelief. The heavy period of rain that had preceded the attack had made the ground so soft that duds were not an altogether unusual occurrence.

In our extremely exposed situation and with the intensity of the fire increasing as the column crept slowly along the roadway, the shelter of the buildings ahead was a welcome sight. The tanks would move, then sit and fire both cannon and machine guns, repeating the process over and over again every few yards.

When we finally reached the first building on the right side of the road, a few of us made a dash for the shelter of its walls. Fortunately, we were then sheltered from the fierce small arms and automatic weapons fire that poured on us from the low ridge. We waited in the walled barnyard for awhile during which time the tanks fired ahead of us down the main street of the village.

Some of us made our way slowly into the village, in the rear of the houses and farms along the main street. I entered a building from the rear, which happened to be a bakery. As I ran heavily across the storeroom, sitting on a chair in front of me was a German soldier. As I approached him, he suddenly slid from the chair onto the floor, literally at my feet. It happened that he was already dead, but the movement of my running dislodged him from the chair and caused him to fall. What a terrifying experience that was!

As I left the bakery, diagonally across the street at the intersection of a road that ran to the south, toward the ridge that was so heavily defended, was a small chapel. I ran across the street toward the chapel and was joined by a new man by the name of Joe. We immediately ran to the house adjoining the chapel, and once inside, there was a violent explosion. A tank had pulled up beside the house we were in and fired the cannon. The concussion shook the house so violently that plaster dropped from the ceiling.

Joe and I then proceeded down the left side of the street, house to house. We came to a small bungalow-type. We burst into the front door, cleared the first floor and were shocked by the disarray in which we found the house. Everything was upside down and not because of war damage. Someone had ransacked the house. Dresser drawers were on the floor with the contents scattered about. What was shocking about the sight was that we were the first Americans to enter the house. Therefore, those who had ransacked the house must have been German soldiers who had occupied the village in its defense.

After clearing the downstairs, we immediately ran upstairs. Because of all the artillery fire, all of the windows were blown out. We came to a side window and looked down and there was a German soldier crawling on his hands and knees along a fence. He was no more than twenty feet from us. He must have been crawling to a bunker which was located in the rear of the property. So quickly that I did not have a chance to respond, or interfere, the man with me raised his rifle and shot the German soldier. I was absolutely shocked.

The German soldier was on his hands and knees, completely helpless and with two rifles focused on him. To shoot a man in such a circumstance was, to me, unconscionable. He should have, by all means, been taken prisoner. But this was Joe's first experience in combat and I was not convinced that even that was an acceptable excuse for what had been done. But immediately after he fired that deadly shot, he was exuberant and said that he couldn't wait to write home to his sons and tell them that he shot a German. I thought that to shoot a helpless man is not an achievement to boast about; especially when I thought of the many times some of us had placed ourselves at the risk to assure taking prisoners.

The entire column came to a halt in front of the house that Joe and I had just cleared and occupied. Joe and I took a position on the second floor at the rear of the house, overlooking the bunker in the garden to the rear of the house. We had been there just a short time when we witnessed an incredible sight. An American medical half-track with the large Red Cross emblazoned on its side and the Red Cross flags fluttering from both fenders, went racing across that deadly open field toward the distant houses of Hastenrath.

There was an eerie lull in the firing in deference to the mission of mercy on which the half-track was embarked. I was overcome with a deep and profound longing that this astonishing moment of quiet would continue. But that was not to be. Sometime later, the half-track emerged from the cover of the buildings with its rescued wounded and that priceless moment of serenity evaporated and the firing resumed.

In front of the house, because of the narrowness of the street, that roadway became a veritable shooting gallery. The tanks hugged the walls of the houses as tightly as possible with only one consolation, and that was there was no possibility of a flank shot.

A short time later, Joe and I were ordered to join the rest of the men in a house directly across the street, since darkness was setting in and there would be no more forward progress. I thought how tragic that we had come such a short distance after all of those hours of deadly combat. How tragic.

Standing Guard

This house that we now occupied was the deepest point we had penetrated into the village of Scherpenseel. A space of about forty feet separated us from the next house on the same side of the street.

Behind the house that we now occupied, there was a shed and a machine gun position was set up next to it. There was a small gully that lay between our position and the heavily defended ridge to the rear of our house. In front of our house, giving us no small comfort, sat a Sherman tank.

The guard roster was made up and tension began to rise to a very high pitch. The inevitable shelling began, for a while evenly distributed between both sides, but then the crescendo of our artillery increased and kept up through most of the night with the primary attention given to the ridge behind our house. Some of the shells seemed barely to clear the roof of our house.

Earlier in the evening, Fred Suedemier and Charles Craig had been doing their assigned tour of guard duty on the machine gun by the shed. After their two hour stint was completed, they were relieved by another team and Fred and Charles came back into the house, into the kitchen where a number of us were huddled.

The scene that then took place was an eruption of unequaled proportions. I have known few men with the temper and the colorful vocabulary that Fred Suedemier possessed. He must have touched base with every vulgarity ever uttered by human tongue. He circled around that kitchen, livid with rage. No one dared to interrupt him to find the cause for this scalding outburst. He finally delivered himself of the offending matter.

Poor Charles Craig, a big, affable, gentle, scholarly man had committed the unpardonable offense. With tension at the ultimate pitch on that guard post by the machine gun, the noise of the shelling making hearing extremely difficult, Craig had the temerity to eat, or rather chew, on Charms, those multi-colored, square Life Savers. In the immortal, unprintable words of Suedemier, "Craig kept chompin' on them blankety, blankety, blank Charms, I couldn't hear a blankety, blank thing. Those blankety, blank Germans could have crawled into our hip pockets before we would have heard them."

He swore that he would never again pull guard with Craig, whereupon Craig had the audacity to be completely unrepentant. This sent another torrent of obscenities spiraling toward the ceiling. When in all of history were such a few benign, colored pieces of hard candy cause for such a tidal wave of vitriolic scorn as were unleashed in that kitchen that night in Scherpenseel?

Sometime in the early hours of the morning, Suedemier asked me to join him on that machine gun post. I immediately emptied my pockets of all Charms and instead, took several sticks of chewing gum and did some of the quietest chewing ever recorded.

As we sat behind the machine gun, the ridge we were facing was still being shelled by our own artillery with unrelenting fury. Straining to hear under those circumstances plays havoc with the nervous system. We were not on guard more than half an hour when heavy firing tore through the night a few yards behind us. There was one of the boldest and most daring counter-attacks I had ever seen taking place right up the main street behind us. The tank in front of the house had a shell in the chamber of the cannon, when somehow, a shot was fired into the barrel and the shell was detonated, causing severe casualties and damaging the tank.

An Impossible Dilemma

Suedemier and I were in an impossible dilemma as we couldn't switch the gun toward the street in case there was a coordinated attack coming up out of the gully, which was no more than fifty yards in front of our position. We could do nothing but hold fast to our position, feeling very vulnerable, with our backs to the fierce action taking place in the street, just a few yards to our rear. However, remarkably, one German soldier made it up the street, past a number of our tanks, as far as the Chapel where he was finally cut down. Unfortunately, his body would lie there for days before being removed.

After a tense, unnerving, action-filled night, we again resumed the attack after daylight. As we moved down the street, we passed a house that must have served as an Aid Station. There were a number of bodies of dead German soldiers, all of them bandaged, lying in a neat row in front of the house.

As we approached the lower end of the village of Scherpenseel, the road made a 90 degree turn toward Hastenrath. However, we took a short cut, moving through an orchard to gain the rear of the houses in Hastenrath. The short cut turned out to be quite perilous. There was a knocked out German vehicle midway between the last building of Scherpenseel and the first house of Hastenrath. One at a time we made the dash, first to the shelter of the damaged vehicle, and then, after getting our breath, we would run as quickly as possible to the other side.

Every time someone moved, there were immediately two quick rounds dropped in on the heels of the dashing soldiers. We knew that someone had perfect observation of everything we did. Fortunately, our squad made it across without incident. We then began working our way through the rear of the houses and out-buildings, clearing them as we went.

At this time I had teamed up with a man by the name of Aloysius

Kampa. The tanks were also moving up cautiously behind us with sporadic cannon and machine gun fire. Their flank was perilously exposed to the German anti-tank guns located on the ridge to our left front.

Al and I entered one house, cleared the first floor and then dashed upstairs. There were plank type doors to the rooms, and one at a time we cleared the second floor. While we were doing that, we heard men entering the house on the first floor below us. Just as Al and I had finished clearing the rooms upstairs, we began to descend the stairs when there was an ugly explosion in the room at the foot of the stairs. There were a number of men wounded and there was a great deal of excitement and consternation trying to figure out what had happened. Some thought a booby-trap had been sprung, others suspected that one of our tanks might have mistakenly or accidentally fired into the house.

Some of the men went charging out to the tanks, accusing them of having fired, but they all vehemently insisted that they had not fired the shot. Al and I didn't linger, probably still in shock in having missed that awful explosion by a mere few seconds.

We continued advancing with another team, leap-frogging from house to house. We knew that the German troops were no more than a house or two ahead of us.

By this time, we had advanced quite a bit ahead of the tanks and we came to an opening of about 75 feet between houses. Just as we came to the opening, we saw several German soldiers disappear into a low shed diagonally across the street from where we were. Again, this time, only three of us made the dash, one at a time, across the opening, now having certain knowledge as to where, at least, some of the enemy troops were. The three of us, after making that scary dash, threw ourselves down behind a pile of rubble to the rear of a house that had a large gaping hole in the foundation. This opening gave us perfect sight of the shed into which the German soldiers had taken up position.

Al and I immediately began firing into the door and windows of that shed. Since it was in an isolated position, we knew that they could not escape from the shed unobserved. There was still much action behind us, both from small arms and also the tanks firing machine guns and cannon intermittently. The third man with us did not do any firing, instead, he launched into a tirade against Al and me for firing. He said we should stop firing, since by firing we were giving away our position. He had the foolish notion that if we didn't shoot at them, they wouldn't shoot at us.

Al and I insisted that since there were men moving up behind us, we had the responsibility to give them covering fire because we knew exactly where the enemy soldiers were. The argument got altogether nasty as Al and I tried to keep our attention on the shed and at the same time arguing over our shoulders with our bitter antagonist.

There was a wall about seven feet high and about twelve feet long that extended out behind the house, separating it from the adjoining house. Suddenly, two German soldiers appeared from around the wall and stood behind us with their hands raised. I immediately got up and approached the first man who was probably in his mid thirties.

He very nervously pointed to his tunic pocket, indicating that he wanted to retrieve something from it. I nodded my head to him and he proceeded to pull out a wallet from inside his pocket. With an excited laugh, he opened his wallet and began showing me photographs. There is nothing like a family photograph to break down barriers and open the hearts of friend and foe alike. Because of his earnestness and his awful state of fear and also his eager attempt to ingratiate himself to us, I was embarrassed into joining him in this grand tour of his photo collection.

What a picture we made! A German and an American soldier looking at family photographs as he identified his wife and his children. There we both stood on a pile of rubble with the full fury and the din of battle raging around us.

That pleasant, heart-warming moment, that humane interlude, had an unpleasant interruption. During that short space of time, one of our men made an attempt to cross the open space and was immediately shot. This completely confirmed what Al and I had been insisting concerning suppressing fire, but what a price to pay.

Caught in the Center

After we had been there for quite some time and had now been joined by others, word came up to us that our squad, or rather, the remnant of our squad was to return to the rest of the platoon. We were within, perhaps, 100 yards of the church in Hastenrath, which may have been the boundary between our unit and the 104th, the "Timberwolves" Division.

Because of the heavy resistance, both the 1st Division, or the "Big Red One", on our right and the "Timberwolves", on our left, had difficulty leaving their line of departure, leaving us in a very exposed position.

It was suddenly very gratifying to hear the sound of heavy machine gun fire on our left, indicating that the 104th was making progress as it came storming over the ridge behind us and to our left. It sounded as though every man in the division had a machine gun and every blessed one was in action.

The few of us carefully made our way through the back yards of the houses that we had earlier taken. Since only the one side of the street had been cleared, the trip back was still quite perilous. Crossing the area that was under direct sight of the school house was particularly unnerving.

By this time, it was getting dark and with that, every shadow becomes ominous. We made our way up the street of Scherpenseel and then our squad was taken down the side street directly opposite the chapel. This street led us toward that infamous, heavily defended ridge. The house we were led to was the last house in the village, facing the dangerous ridge.

That ridge was in the area of the 1st Division responsibility and they were still a distance from taking it. But with the 104th to our left rear, and the "Big Red One" to our right rear, we were like a finger pushing into the belly of the enemy; vulnerable on both sides and in front.

Our situation in Scherpenseel was still so tenuous that open movement from Werth to Scherpenseel, or even down the street to our house during daylight hours, was deadly. Between the high ground to the north of the village and the similar high ground to the south of Scherpenseel and adding to that, the excellent observation post the Germans possessed in the Hastenrath school house, absolutely no movement went unnoticed, but was subjected to every form of fire.

Since we had moved into our new position during darkness, we had no idea of the serious nature of our situation. There was a house-barn combination directly across from the house we occupied and for some reason none of our people were positioned there, which seemed to be the logical thing to do for our support and protection, but who were we to remonstrate?

We immediately placed a 30 caliber machine gun in the first floor window. This gave us a field of fire covering the nearest part of the ridge. After dark, there was a tank brought down the street and through a narrow alley way between the last two houses and took a position behind our house where it did absolutely no good. The tankers not on duty occupied the other part of the rather small house. In the front room of the house where the machine gun was located, there was a trap door in the floor leading to the cellar and a very small cellar it was.

Since the second floor was pretty severely damaged, we did not use it for sleeping quarters. The first night we slept in the cellar and the cellar was so small that I decided to sleep in the potato bin. It did not help that I was claustrophobic! The next night, I would have no part of the cellar, so several of us slept on the kitchen floor.

During our first morning in that position, one of the men on the machine gun called to us to come to the window. He pointed to the ridge. There was a German soldier standing upright in his foxhole, stretching, and then he stooped down, picked up his overcoat and in plain sight of all, began to put it on. We were all amazed because he was so clearly outlined against the horizon. The next morning he did the very same thing. However, this time one of our men, who must have been at an upstairs window, shot him. It was such a pathetic sight that we truly hoped he was only wounded.

The evening of the second day we were in that position, we acquired some sorely needed replacements. One of the men, named Wertman came through the door of the kitchen and there were only about three or four words out of his mouth when I recognized the unmistakable Pennsylvania German accent. In fact, he lived about 30 miles from my home. Another man by the name of Burdulis, a decidedly scholarly looking man, a former school teacher and the father of two girls, also joined us. Another man who had joined us, Fred Dorsey, from South Carolina, who unfortunately, could neither read nor write, was part of the large group of the "Scherpenseel Replacements".

Later on, while those of us who were not on guard duty on the machine gun sat on the kitchen floor getting acquainted with the new men, the door burst open and in stormed a man like a raging bull. His face was horribly flushed and his eyes were fierce and wild. There was no mistaking that he was terribly drunk. Somehow, along the way he must have acquired some medical alcohol. He was completely deranged and he held his rifle on us, threatening to kill anyone who moved. This terrifying stand-off must have lasted at least fifteen of the longest minutes of our lives. He finally moderated and we were able to talk with him and convince him to lower his rifle. That man survived the war, but how, we can't even begin to imagine.

That was also the night, when for the first time, we were issued sleeping bags. These were merely form-fitting G.I. blankets with a water repellent cover. The top of the sleeping bag covered the head like a hood. My first night in the sleeping bag was a complete nightmare. After crawling into the sleeping bag, I zipped it up and went to sleep. During the night I awakened and didn't know where

I was, since somehow I had turned around in the sleeping bag and was facing the rear of the hood. I was seized with my ongoing claustrophobia and had a serious panic attack. No more of the stuff. After that, I folded the hood down and used it as a pillow.

It was the third day when the 1st Division finally came abreast of us and passed beyond us, finally freeing us from the menace of that dreaded ridge. That troublesome piece of real estate that caused us considerable trouble and so many casualties must have looked like Swiss cheese from the air, because of the fearsome artillery bombardment it had sustained.

We had finally been bypassed by both the 104th and the "Big Red One", effectively pinching us out of the action, since we had accomplished our mission of creating the breakthrough. We were finally able to relax somewhat and breathe a little easier. The front had moved so dramatically that they even brought the kitchen forward and placed it in Scherpenseel. It was proof positive that we really had a kitchen, contrary to what we had come to believe. Unfortunately, the kitchen was placed near where the Aid Station had been, with all of the dead bodies.

A Brief Tranquility

Life in Scherpenseel now changed dramatically. The tranquility we now enjoyed in Scherpenseel was like an anesthetic. We could now observe life unharried and uninterrupted.

It seemed that the German monsoon season was still in progress. The main street in Scherpenseel, although pockmarked from all of the artillery damage and each hole water-filled, I was able to make some cogent observations. First; it was gratifying to watch all of the traffic now moving up to the battle front, using the very street where you had been among the first to free from the enemy's hold and remembering how foreboding that street looked. You just felt that all of those vehicles were driving down that street through the courtesy of all of your efforts and risk and sacrifice.

The second observation that I made was that I could almost immediately distinguish between the "old men" in the company, as opposed to the new men who had just joined us. When it came to all of those water-filled holes, as the men walked toward the kitchen, it was interesting to note that the old men simply walked right through those water-filled holes, without deviating a step, whereas, the new men, carefully walked around them. What a philosophical story that tells us as to what happens to men who have been in combat.

Life in Scherpenseel took on a whole unreal atmosphere, one that we were completely unused to; this new life was the total province of the "rear echelon".

A good friend of mine, Ross Overholt and I found a chicken in the barnyard across the street, with its feet tied together. We immediately scoured the village for chicken feed. We came across a barrel in a nearby house and "liberated" it. This was not really an act of compassion for the chicken. Rather, we envisioned a fresh chicken dinner. In fact, the chicken became rather attached to us so that it followed us around. It is not altogether flattering to be followed around by a chicken. This dalliance did not last long, because one day the chicken disappeared along with the dream of a chicken dinner. Someone had stolen our dream.

The "tankers" who shared the house with us told us how they longed to get hold of some M-1's since all they had were those wretched "grease guns". Very dutifully, I spent time going over the battlefield and gathered about seven or eight rifles. I carried the kitchen table outside behind the house and set up for the business of cleaning the rifles. I carefully field stripped each one, cleaned them, oiled them and then reassembled each one. I had all the rifles lying on the table for their final checking and for some reason I had walked away. Sometime later, I returned and Ross Overholt came out of the kitchen and was standing in the doorway of the house.

We were engaged in a conversation as I picked up the rifles, one at a time, pulled the bolt back, pulled the trigger, laid it down, picked up the next one and so on, all the while during our conversation. I picked up the last rifle, pulled the bolt back and pulled the trigger and to my horror the gun fired and hit the wall of the house about three feet over Ross's head. What a frightening moment that was! During my absence, for some reason, someone had laid their loaded rifle right alongside the ones I had just finished cleaning. What a painful lesson that was.

Our stay in Scherpenseel was becoming quite pleasant and we decided to make things as comfortable as possible. We decided to put the kitchen stove in our kitchen back into service, so we began searching for coal. In the farm house across the street we came across a small pile of the coal briquettes. We transferred the coal to our house and made ourselves comfortable.

Then, the inevitable day came when we were ordered to load up on our half-tracks. The holiday was over. We left Scherpenseel sometime after we had just gotten more new men. It turned out to be a very interesting and informative ride. Those new men could not have joined us at a worse time and place because the battle field around Scherpenseel and Hastenrath was a classic picture of the death and destruction of war.

There were the charred hulks of burned out Sherman tanks, of which there were many. There were the bodies of many German soldiers strewn around the field or in the foxholes they had occupied. Near one knocked out Sherman tank, there was a GI boot with a foot still in it.

There was one new man who had taken a tour of the battlefield and returned very shaken by the number of dead. The man's name was Boyer, from North Carolina and he always spoke through clenched teeth. In his classic southern vernacular, a very frightened man said, "Them dead Germans is so many as piss ants."

In the darkened half-track, one of the men, George Sampson, began regaling us with stories. George turned out to be the consummate story teller. That night George, who to me was a total stranger, began telling about some of his romantic escapades and in the course of his story telling, I found out that George was from Allentown, Pa., just five miles from Emmaus, where I lived. He began talking about a girl named Julie. I was stunned; he was talking about a neighbor girl. Fortunately, his story was completely respectable.

The half-track finally stopped and we were told to dismount and form up. We must have marched about an hour through the darkness. At one point we saw a long piece of white marker tape, indicating a mine field. Sometime later we were told that we had been led on the wrong side of the tape, actually walking through the mine field. How reassuring!

We finally arrived at a compound of some type and this compound was adjacent to a heavily damaged castle; a castle, complete with a moat. The place was a bloody mess with American bodies scattered around. One poor dead GI had his face partially consumed by some pigs that were let loose.

We were in a holding position. There was an upset Panther tank right by one of our guard positions, a real reminder of the presence and power of the enemy. Holding positions might sound uneventful; however, you can never let down your guard. The German soldier is not only a bold soldier, but a very resourceful one.

The position we were guarding was Frenzburg Castle. The place had been defended by the German 3rd Parachute Division and was finally taken by the 9th Infantry Division. One of their men won the Congressional Medal of Honor for his actions in crossing the moat to the castle, having breached the main entrance almost single-handed.

There was a rather interesting elderly lady who resided in the main house. She insisted that, in fact and indeed, she was a real German princess. We nodded in agreement, but inwardly, we were not altogether persuaded.

After about two days, we again made the trek through the area of the mine field, but this time on the right side of the tape.

On our way back, we spent the night in Weisweiler, simply stopping along the way and going into the nearest house. What was memorable to me was that we spent the night in a house with the entire front of the house blown out, and there, exposed to all of the elements, was a beautiful grand piano. What a waste.

It was like coming home when we returned to Scherpenseel. Those of us who had participated in taking the village, looked upon it as our own, our very own private oasis.

This time, however, we were located in another house, in fact, the same house where, during our first night in the village, Suedemier had given his "Command Performance" with his explosive epithets directed at poor Craig.

The time we spent in Scherpenseel, with the arrival of the new men, helped to bind us together as a real fighting unit. It was far better than having men join while the unit is engaged in combat and there is not time, really, to assimilate men properly into a unit. Our next combat mission would be that of men who had come to know and respect and enjoy each other.

It was from those Scherpenseel replacements that I would meet, not only two of the finest men I have known, but also men who would embody all of those great attributes that would carry on and even enhance the reputation of a division that would emblazon its name in the annals of history. Of the men who had joined our squad that night in the Scherpenseel kitchen, three of them would, in the very near future, be killed in action. They were Wertman, Dorsey and Burdulis.

Two of the other men who joined our squad in Scherpenseel, Harry Clark and George Sampson, would distinguish themselves as real combat leaders, each one, after the "Bulge", commanding a squad. George would win the Silver Star for incredible bravery, after I had been wounded at Sterpigny and later he would win the Bronze star for another feat of courage. Harry Clark would also distinguish himself, also winning the Bronze Star, after having been wounded.

Those are the memories and those are the men that made Scherpenseel such an important part of our history.

One cloudy, overcast day, the air was suddenly filled with the sound of high performance engines; fighter planes were out in force. The ceiling was quite low and a German FW-190 came screaming over Hastenrath by itself when a P-38 Lightening dropped through the clouds right behind him and shot him down. The German pilot was able to bail out, but unfortunately, he was dead when he hit the ground. The German plane dove into the ground between the houses of Hastenrath.

What we had witnessed was the German air activity that had spelled the beginning of the "Battle of the Bulge".

It wasn't long before we were in our half-tracks and on our way south to Belgium to write another bloody chapter called "The Battle of the Bulge". Scherpenseel would increasingly become an even more pleasant memory.

The Retaking Of Grandmenil

Overlooking Grandmenil

Claudine Lambert, myself, "Mrs. Gaby"

We left the La Gleize area after having participated with the 30th Division in a blocking action to contain the German Panzer column that was trying to break out to the North. We were Company D, 2nd Battalion, the 36th Armored Infantry Regiment, of the 3rd Armored Division.

The column of half-tracks moved to a new location where the vehicles coiled, regrouped, and waited for the orders to move to our next engagement. It seemed as though we never really knew precisely where we had been, or indeed, where we were at that moment, and certainly not where we were heading. The state of not knowing seemed to be the unchallenged domain of the ordinary Infantryman.

When orders did come to move out, everyone mounted up and our half-track crept slowly onto the roadway and fell into its assigned position in the Company order of march.

Our half-track was D-23 with the name Dracula painted on its side. The significance of that name always defied me, except that it began with the letter D representing Dog Company. The number 23 meant that we were the 2nd Platoon, 3rd Rifle Squad.

The experience of life in the half-track while traveling from one sector of the front to another was an experience of a life with a quality all of its own. It might be, perhaps, more historically desirable to say that this squad of men now moving to its next engagement sat grimly and stoically in two ranks, silently facing each other on those steel seats in the open half-track, blessedly, this is blatantly untrue. In facing the dread of the unknown, one of the most marvelous salves for the pain of the fears, anxieties, and wonderings is the very diversity of human nature itself. It is that diversity with the spontaneous contribution that each individual makes that is in part the secret of the astonishing resilience of the human spirit.

So, when I remember the hours that we had together in that vehicle, they were hours that were very much alive. There was always the reliving of the last battle, but then there would also be the teasing, the arguing, the joking, and usually some horseplay along with the somber moments that each of us in turn would have.

Sgt. Fickel

In the Command position in the front of the half-track stood our Squad Leader, Sgt. Fickel. He was a man whose courage, conduct and performance never gave anyone license to take any liberties whatsoever with his unlikely name. He had a very strong sense of propriety and an equally strong sense of responsibility for his squad. The very qualities that made him a good Squad Leader also had aspects to them that brought amusement, and as is ever true, it is the humorous aspects that we remembered most vividly and enjoyed recounting the most.

In Stolberg, before he became the Squad Leader, Fickel was possibly the assistant. We were holding a house that was in a forward position. The only thing that separated us from the Germans was a glass and debris strewn street with the body of an American soldier lying right in the midst of it all. The machine guns were located in the front windows of the house, while those of us who were not on duty lived and slept in a back room on the second floor. The only accommodations that we had were a table and several chairs, but to the Infantryman, this was sheer luxury. If we sat on a chair, we were not permitted to lean back so that the chair would rest only on the two rear legs. This, Fickel insisted was not only improper, but was also damaging to the furniture, notwithstanding that parts of the house had already been blown out by shell fire and much of the rest of the house was in disarray because of other damage.

To show his concern for our well being, he told us one day that in order to relieve the monotony of our usual rations he would prepare a very special treat. Replacing his steel helmet with a chef's hat, he went rummaging through the 10-in-1 rations that we were issued, along with those of other squads, gathered every candy bar, every cracker, fruit bar and countless other food items, broke them up, mixed them together, and then heated this conglomeration and pronounced it a "Pudding". We were then requested in command tones to eat it. Seated around the table with the four legs of every chair planted firmly on the floor, we ate this treat with varying degrees of enthusiasm.

A short time later we were alerted to move out of this position, that by now we had come to consider a place of luxury. Gathering our gear together, we made our way out of the rear of the house, through the back yards and over numerous fences and then through the ruins of a factory building to our half-tracks. We then moved to some high ground outside of Stolberg. Dismounting, we made our way past huge slag mounds, slipping into water filled shell holes, all the time trying to avoid tripping over what seemed to be miles of communication wire, since by this time darkness had already set in. We entered into a wooded area where we were to relieve another unit, and one by one, the squads were dropped off along the way to their assigned positions until we were the last to be placed.

It must have been one of the dogmatic rules of our Company that the 3rd Rifle Squad must be assigned to the most remote and isolated spot that could be found. By this time we were well inside the woods so that the only way we could keep together was by maintaining actual physical contact because of the unusually dark night. Finally, after many whispered exchanges and many delays, we were finally led two by two to the foxhole assigned us and relieved those men who had occupied it. Fortunately, those whom we had just relieved had left some of their blankets in the bottom of the foxhole. This hole was located at the far edge of the woods area.

Moving into a strange area at night is always a most disconcerting experience because of the tension of not knowing precisely where the enemy is and how and when they will respond. It is then that the imagination really gears up and begins churning out all sorts of possible scenarios. The foxhole assigned to my friend John Emmurian and me was a very shallow log and earth covered hole, barely large enough for one man. Because of the precarious nature of our situation, John and I decided to alternate in sleeping and standing guard. He would sleep first for two hours while I would pull guard, and then he would take his turn.

Fickel's Concoction

As I sat on the edge of the foxhole listening and watching, things began to settle down and become quiet as everyone adjusted to his new position. Sometime later I began to hear the sound of combat boots crushing dried leaves and the sound of breaking twigs from within our defensive position. As time went by, there was the sound of more scurrying about and this alarmed me because it seemed so careless of men who were experienced combat soldiers. I was sure that if this would continue there would shortly be a German flare hanging in the air over us. These sounds not only continued, but the tempo increased and I also began hearing the most uncommon sounds along with some very strange oaths filtering through the darkness. Trying to restrain myself to keep quiet, I thought, "What in the world is going on?"

It was then that I felt a sudden discomfort come over me. And then, just as quickly, I was seized with fiery convulsions in my lower abdominal region. All of a sudden the whole scene became clear; along with my comrades, I had been smitten with what each of us must have been convinced was terminal diarrhea. It was Fickel's devilish concoction! Knowing that I was entrapped inside the webbing and straps of my combat harness, and also knowing that it would take superhuman effort to extricate myself quickly from all that paraphernalia, there was but one thing to do and that was to become momentarily hysterical.

At once all of those uncommon sounds and those very strange oaths not only became understandable, but also quite reasonable. Sometime later as I resumed my guard duties, I felt stirring at my feet and I perceived that John had awakened. There was the sound of movement in the foxhole and heavy breathing as John had evidently been smitten too, and awaking in an unfamiliar place, not knowing immediately where he was, had begun trying to escape from the foxhole. The sound of the struggle became altogether fierce as he tried to untangle himself from the GI blankets and make his exit. Then there was quiet followed shortly with the most pathetic and lamentable groans of dismay one could ever hear.

As the sun rose the next morning, it rose on a weary, weakened squad, but, remarkably, a squad that in these few hours of arriving in a completely strange position, now defended ground that had already been thoroughly reconnoitered. Every foot of ground within that position was now completely familiar by virtue of the numerous compelling excursions made across that treacherous landscape. For that memorable night, Sgt. Fickel would not soon be forgotten.

Fellow Soldiers

Fred Dorsey was a quiet South Carolinian who had the great misfortune of not being able to read or write. This meant that he would have to constantly humiliate himself and ask someone to read to him the letters from his wife. It would not be an unusual sight to see Fred huddled with someone in the corner of the half-track to help him with his letters. He would take one of us quietly aside and we would then read to him those letters from his wife; loving words in which all their dreams and hopes and desires were shared, and we could not help but feel like embarrassed intruders in that sacred and intimate province that belong to husband and wife alone.

Fred seemed always to be occupied with a leather holster that he was making for a pistol that he had. Almost every spare moment would find him working on it with an intensity that was almost unnatural. I doubt whether that holster was ever finished, because within a short span of time, Fred would be lying beside a dirty black hole in the snow where the last earthly sound that he would hear was the whisper of that falling mortar shell.

There was no man that could orchestrate the feelings of everyone in the squad, as could George Sampson. He could plunge us into the very depths of the gloom of homesickness by simply reaching into his inside pocket and pulling out his small harmonica and playing for us some melancholy tune. And just as quickly we could be laughing and singing to one of the many novelty songs that he knew and of which he seemed to have an unending repertoire.

Charles Craig was a large and gentle Missourian who found it impossible to be either impolite or discourteous, but that gentleness could explode into fearlessness if the situation arose. However, Charles made one serious error when he told us that he had studied geology while in college. We would take great delight in reminding him how eminently qualified he was to be an

Infantryman, since digging holes in the earth was one of our majors too.

Harry Clark was the family man in the squad. Coming from Alabama, he was also our beloved Rebel. His voice would rise in octaves as well as decibels as he would be constantly forced to parry the thrust of supposed Yankee wit. (His particular nemesis in this matter would usually be Jack Buss.) Harry always enjoyed telling us about his football exploits in his high school days, and when the occasion arose, he delighted in displaying his dancing prowess with the least possible incitement. When he would break into one of his light-footed jigs, we thought this absolutely remarkable considering his advanced age of thirty-two years.

Although Jack Buss had been wounded at La Gleize, it would be unfair not to mention him at this point because of his contribution, no matter how questionable, to our squad in our half-track experience. Jack was the unquestioned scholar in the squad, and would not let us forget that his college career had been interrupted so that he might be with us. He was also the master provocateur. He seemed to find a strange and perverse delight in making a deliberately outrageous remark, usually in Harry's direction, which he knew would turn that half-track into an inferno of debate, and then he would sit back and joyfully keep the fires of controversy stoked until we who were but the witless, khaki clad dolts had exhausted ourselves, and our miserable arguments. Then he would stretch himself out to his full intellectual stature and with his inestimable knowledge, he would ruthlessly flay this poor, unlearned peasantry whom the misfortunes of war had inflicted upon him.

Traveling in an open half-track in the wintertime is a bone-chilling experience. This fact will bring you face to face with one of the most monumental challenges that you can expect to confront. Sooner or later you will be innocently overcome with the simple desire for a cup of hot coffee. Since convoy travel in combat areas means interminable stops and starts and delays, time to make a cup of coffee should be no real problem-that is until you try it.

Among several of the squad members I was jokingly referred to as the "fastest coffee maker in the Army." If this was a fair reputation, it was one that was earned with much travail and frustration, developed principally during this type of travel.

As soon as the half-track would stop, I would leap out, fill my canteen cup with water, arrange the heating material, and get the fire going. Then I would hunch over this hopeful enterprise, peering into the depths of the cup waiting, coaxingly, for that first bubble that would indicate that the water was starting to heat, all the while looking over my shoulder nervously for any sign of convoy movement. Then invariably, simultaneously, bubbles would begin breaking the surface of the water, there would be excited shouts all along the roadway, engines would begin turning over and half-track doors would begin slamming the full length of the convoy with a rapidity that gave the sound of falling steel dominoes.

Grabbing the searing hot handle of the canteen cup, I would kick out the fire and begin pursuing the escaping half-track, hoping that my friends would not pull the stunt that seemed to bring them an endless source of amusement, and that was to slam the door in my face before I could mount and then watch with glee to see how fast and how far I could run without spilling any of the contents of my cup. When they would finally relent and I would bound on board, I would usually find myself standing in the back of the half-track clutching a cup of lukewarm water. But nevertheless, undaunted, I knew that the next stop would finally bring success and I could finally put my lips to that cup of delicious hot Nescafe coffee.

Are these simply the irrelevant activities, along with the personal idiosyncrasies of a squad of men marking time before being plunged into the next battle, perhaps, unworthy of reciting? No! The sum total of all those things provided those essential ingredients that always served so beautifully to insulate the mind from that unspeakable dread that was ever present, lurking, waiting to overtake and to possess our thinking. As our convoy continued slowly along toward Grandmenil, just before dusk, we came upon a sight that was startling because of the horrible implications of the scene.

In a small wedge-shaped field by the roadway were the hulks of four burned out tanks, two German and two American. These tanks must have met suddenly and in complete surprise in that very small area. They stood there, muzzle-to-muzzle and hull-to-hull, having destroyed each other at point blank range. One can only imagine the horror of those last few seconds as each crew tried frantically to survive such an impossible moment. The unopened hatches were mute testimony to the futility of their desperate actions. One tank stood with a pyramid of molten metal beneath its rear engine compartment, looking as though it were the excrement of the tank itself, as if the vehicle had ingested the white hot metal that had destroyed it and then in its death throes, deposited it on the ground as it died within the perimeter of that small pasture.

Christmas Eve

Darkness now settled over the convoy of half-tracks as it rumbled and screeched its way through the hills and forests of the Ardennes. But as we traveled that night, there was one great, profound truth that began to emerge in all its loftiness and with all its triumph. This was Christmas Night, and this great truth is that there is absolutely nothing that can overpower that indomitable spirit of Christmas. Neither the fresh recollections of our engagement at La Gleize, with its inevitable casualties, nor that ugly scene of those four charred, armored mausoleums as they stood silently on that postage stamp size battlefield, nor the dread anticipation of what lay ahead in the darkness, could suppress the joy of Christmas, because somehow we found ourselves in the cold darkness of that open half-track standing and singing Christmas carols.

We approached the wooded ridge overlooking the village of Grandmenil in the early evening. The convoy of half-tracks left the roadway and began coiling among the trees, while we on board hurriedly gathered our equipment and prepared to dismount. What lexicon is adequate to describe the feelings that a soldier endures in the silent turmoil of his own heart when he approaches this moment. The unreal world of that half-track would now be translated into the harsh, ugly, reality of war, with the shouts, the explosions, the screams, and that almost terrifying staccato of the German Schmeiser machine-pistol.

After falling out on the roadway, there was the usual milling around, with both Noncoms and Officers darting back and forth as last minute arrangements were made. Each of us was wondering about the real nature of the mission, and at the same time also, confident that we would find nothing out about it.

Finally, after what seemed to be ceaseless waiting, the tanks began positioning themselves at intervals along the roadway, and then sat with their engines idling. While the Infantry was waiting to move out, we knew that our 2nd Platoon would follow the lead platoon which would either be the 1st or the 3rd, giving us some solace that would not last for more than a few minutes.

Grandmenil

As the signal was given to move forward, the column began emerging from the cover of the woods. Ahead of us was a long descending roadway with the village of Grandmenil lying at the foot, already on fire from the artillery shells that were falling into it and the reports of the explosions echoing back and forth across the valley.

One of the most irritating things for an Infantryman, who must work with tanks, especially at night when a quiet approach was so essential in the attack, was the incessant screeching of the bogey wheels of the tank. This sound was so loud and aggravating, even drowning out the noise of the tank engine, that you were convinced that every German soldier within a radius of 500 yards had now been alerted, and each one of them was peering over his rifle aimed directly at you. Nevertheless, in spite of that grievance, the very silhouette of that grotesque looking steel companion, with its cannon jutting like a feeler out into the darkness, was a very comforting sight, if not sound.

To the right of the road there rose a rather steep wooded embankment, which fell off ahead of us quite abruptly down to road level. On the left side of the road was an equally sharp drop off. The embankment to our right served one negative purpose in that it robbed us of that split second warning that incoming artillery fire gives. In an instant, the roadway was erupting with exploding shells. Fortunately, there was a rather deep ditch on the right of the road where some of us found shelter. The volume of incoming fire was astonishing, and what compounded the awfulness of it was that it was our own artillery falling short. The dismay and the anger that one feels in such an ordeal are inexpressible. With shells falling in so fast and so close that the very heat could be felt, the feeling of helplessness is maddening.

Tank Commanders could be heard over all of this noise screaming into their radios to lift the fire because it was falling on our own men. Cries and angry screams were rising all along the column, and especially among the forward platoon, which caught the brunt of the fire. The casualties among that lead platoon were so substantial that it could no longer function in the lead capacity, and our platoon passed through it and all the carnage that the damaging fire had inflicted on that lead element.

The column again began to move forward toward the village. By this time the embankment to our right disappeared to road level, and now, in fact, the roadway was built up several feet above the level of the adjoining fields.

With our squad now in the lead position and our Platoon Sgt. Pop Waters at the very front, Pop gave the signal for the column to stop. He had noticed what appeared to be an outpost position dug into the side of the road embankment.

Pop Waters was an extraordinary soldier who did almost everything unconventionally. We suspected that he was never issued a steel helmet, because all he ever wore was the G.I. wool knit cap, and all that the cap covered was a rim of reddish hair around his balding head. Before combat, back in Normandy, he had been a Pfc. BAR man who had a reputation for not caring too very much about anything, much less the rigors of military discipline and routine. But as the Division moved from the Normandy Beachhead to the Siegfried Line, Pop also moved from Pfc. to Platoon Sgt. Pop was one of those rare men with intuitive sense that some men, without any benefit of leadership training, come by so easily and naturally. No matter what the circumstances, it seemed he instinctively had the right response along with the courage to execute what needed to be done. He was a legend in the Company, but unfortunately never received proper recognition. It was a most reassuring sight to see that little guy with the wool knit cap, because then we knew all was well.

When the column stopped, Pop took two men with him, George Sampson and Aloysius Kampa, down off the roadway to the field level where the outpost was. Dug into the embankment was a hole in which two German soldiers sat sleeping with their rifles locked upright between their knees. Pop simply reached in with a hand on each rifle barrel and jerked them from their grasp. One soldier reacted in such an animated manner that Kampa interpreted his movements as hostile and shot him dead. The other man was taken prisoner in a state of absolute panic.

The column again resumed its movement which would carry it the final 200 yards to the village. By this time our squad had now spread out around the lead tank, with some of our men on both sides of the tank. In such situations, tension begins mounting to levels that are almost unbearable because you have no illusions that you will simply walk into the village uncontested. Very quickly the tension was broken with the unearthly scream of direct fire and a shattering explosion with an earsplitting metallic ring, as the lead tank was hit. The driver immediately threw the tank into reverse, and those who survived the hit began trying to escape the doomed vehicle. With the tank in reverse, it careened backwards off to the right of the roadway with me in its path, desperately trying to get out of its way.

It is a most frightening experience to be caught in the path of an abandoned, out of control, 32-ton monster that is bearing down on you. After the tank left the roadway, it circled in tight circles in the adjoining field and then burned. To the left of the tank, at impact, was Charles Craig. In trying to get out of the line of fire, he jumped into a hole beside the road, which happened to be occupied by a German soldier, whom he shot dead.

The squad, being without its tank, moved off the left side of the roadway about 20 or 30 yards, to the dark shadows of a hedge line, waiting to decide what to do. We were there only a very short time when an officer approached us; it happened to be Major McGeorge. Several of us had been at his side one time during the La Gleize action as he stood by while several of his tanks were destroyed on a roadway that was impossible for them to leave to avoid the fire. We remembered the agony of that man as he counted the survivors of those tanks on that day, and, we saw the genuiness of that officer. Remarkably, at this time, he asked us if we would not join the other tanks because they needed the Infantry support.

This Major asked us, he didn't order us, but the earnestness of his plea was more forceful than any command could possibly have been. He also told us that he would reorganize the attack and have the tanks leave the roadway and move in abreast in the final rush to the village. This was done with one tank to the left of the roadway and the other three tanks off to the right of the roadway, moving at a rush to the first buildings at the edge of the village. The tanks moved rapidly, delivering a heavy fusillade of fire as they made that final lunge to the village, with the Infantry following close behind. Our squad was dispersed among those tanks on the right of the intersection, with the foundation walls of those first houses as our line, also extending off to the right along a fence line. The firing was very intense, with cannon, machine-gun and rifle fire being poured into the village, intermixed with the responding German fire.

Fred Suedemier

One man who made his mark early in this action was a man who constantly boasted as to how much he hated the Germans. Whenever we were close enough to their position, he took great delight in shouting his feelings to them in the loudest and most colorful language. He was a good, reliable, and completely unselfish soldier. After I had been wounded in Normandy, I returned to our Company just after they entered Germany in early September. As of then, till some time later, all I had to wear was the old, flimsy field jacket. The weather became quite a bit colder and uncomfortable as the weeks went by. One night when we were in position outside of Stolberg, this man disappeared from our position; several hours later he reappeared and without a word, simply threw a mackinaw at me. I found out later that he had crawled out into a "no man's land" area, which was under constant fire, to one of our knocked out tanks, located this mackinaw and crawled back with it. His name was Fred Suedemier.

Fred had his moment this night when a group of German soldiers was found to be in a small depressed area between some of the foundations just ahead of us. With fires in the village flaring and then dying and flaring again, it was at times possible to catch glimpses of some of them trying to flee to a more rearward position. Suedemier positioned himself prominently on a pile of rubble, and with the ever present trickle of tobacco juice at the corner of his mouth, began shooting and spitting and lecturing at the top of his lungs. He seemed to take particular umbrage at their dietary preferences and also at their hereditary flaws, because he continually taunted them with, "Come on you Kraut eatin' sons of bitches, why don't you come out and fight?"

What with Suedemier's performance and a feeling that we were in a pretty strong position, there was a rather light hearted atmosphere among us, especially after we had been there some time and someone called our attention to one house to our right rear that seemed to have been relatively untouched. The question was asked if anyone had checked out that house, and it was found that no one had been in it. A few men then entered it and in a short time emerged with at least ten or twelve German prisoners who had been in there all the while.

There was quite a bit of joking and laughing as this party of prisoners was formed up to be taken back to the rear. After that was taken care of, several of us took a position lying behind a small earthen mound by the fence line to the right of the destroyed houses. As we lay there, there was an instant of activity right behind us. Then someone spurted right between us and with a few wild leaps disappeared into the darkness in front of us. This must have been one member of that party that had surrendered who had decided to make a run for it, and the fact that the action developed behind us caught us so totally by surprise that not a shot was fired.

At about this very same time we heard a commotion behind us and found out that a new company was moving in behind us. It was a Company of the 75th Division. The fact that they were a new unit became quickly identifiable because of the way they were setting up. As the commands were shouted about, everyone was being addressed most formally. It was Sgt. so and so, Cpl. this and Cpl. that, and this gave the whole setting somewhat of a Basic Training atmosphere. This, too, added to what turned out to be a totally unwarranted feeling of confidence and light heartedness in our situation at the time.

Ahead of us we could hear the sound of vehicle movement, an indication that the Germans were about ready to make their move. It sounded as though they were attempting to bring a tank around to our right flank where, if successful, it could have been extremely damaging. Our Platoon Leader, Lt. Mellitz, recognized this and called for the bazooka team, which happened to be George Sampson and me. He told us that he wanted us to move up the roadway, which ran off to the right, and to position ourselves so as to be ready to intercept the tank if it approached us from that direction. As George and I moved out, we passed another bazooka team and I tried unsuccessfully to cajole them to go with us to back us up in case the first shot missed; this they declined to do. But no sooner had we reached a suitable place when we were recalled.

Lt. Mellitz

Occupying the tank on the left side of the intersection as we entered the edge of the village was an officer by the name of Capt. Jordan. He had ordered Lt. Mellitz to have our unit push further into the village. When George and I returned to the spot where Lt. Mellitz was, along with other members of our squad, we found out about these new orders. As we waited there to form up, there was a further exchange between Jordan and Mellitz. Mellitz called over to Jordan and asked him if he intended to send his tanks with us. Jordan replied that they would not be going with us, whereupon Mellitz asked, "Then what will we have for support?" Jordan responded, "You have your rifles!" The reply that Mellitz then made would become his epitaph. "I'll do it, but I don't like it!" Within less than five minutes after he uttered that remark, he would be dead.

After that conversation between Mellitz and Jordan, Lt. Mellitz formed us up and he led off with several men on the left side of the street and a few of us on the right, in the opening stages of this new attack. We hadn't moved more than a few yards down both sides of the street into the village when there was an explosion of unusual force. It must have been a round of high explosive from a nearby German tank. That shell left Lt. Mellitz dead, as well as a man by the name of Lester Wertman, and a number of our men wounded, so the attack never really got under way.

George Sampson must have been hit by a piece of flying debris that struck him in the arm with such force that it knocked his rifle out of his grasp. Convinced that his arm was broken, he made his way back to where Sgt. Fickel was, and reported his condition. Hoping against hope that his arm really was broken, was a short lived expectation because Sgt. Fickel told him to raise his arm, and when Sampson obediently raised it, Fickel informed him that his diagnosis was faulty, since he could not possibly have raised it if it had been broken. Sampson immediately compounded his problem by informing Fickel that he had lost his rifle in the course of that action, when it was blown from his grasp, and he wasn't sure exactly where it was. Sgt. Fickel told him in no uncertain terms that the rifle was his full responsibility and no matter where it was, Sampson would have to retrieve it or suffer the consequences. By now the tank fire was supplemented with machine gun fire that was raking the street through which Sampson would have to crawl in order to find that errant rifle. Picking his way through the rubble, in the face of the continued fire, this good and obedient soldier somehow found it and brought this treasure back to display to his pleased Squad Leader.

It was quite obvious that the round fired from that tank was the opening phase of what would certainly be a German counter attack, because we could sense the initiative being assumed by the Germans. Within a short time, in addition to the machine gun firing a grazing fire down the main street of the village, there was a gun that opened up on our left flank, and shortly thereafter another off to our right front. The fire from these flank guns converged behind us. The firing escalated considerably with direct fire now being thrown at tanks to the right side of the intersection, and within a short time the three were damaged to the point of being unusable. Our squad, by this time, had taken up positions inside the rubble filled foundation walls of the house in front of those disabled tanks. It seemed now that an all out infantry assault would be imminent. With the intensity of the fire, our position soon became untenable, and an order was issued for us to cross the street into the rubble of the foundation of the house directly in front of the tank occupied by Capt. Jordan.

Crossing a street that is covered with machine gun fire is an unenviable prospect, especially when there are four or five men who must cross. The first man might take the enemy by surprise, but after that it can be a deadly situation. One man crossing a street strewn with debris and lots of broken glass makes as much noise as a whole squad under ordinary circumstances. Not being able to get a running start, but having to crawl over a foundation wall and immediately into the street carrying a Bazooka or the bazooka rounds, in addition to the rifle and the other gear, along with that psychological impediment of knowing that you must pass the bodies of your own two comrades as you cross that piece of ground, makes that short expanse seem a mile wide.

Fortunately, the four or five of us who made that dash across the road made it without incident, and joined those few men who were already there. Among those who were there, inside that rubble filled foundation, was also a very badly wounded tanker with a sucking chest wound, who had earlier been dragged from one of the knocked out tanks. Harry Clark and George Sampson helped carry him back for the help that he so desperately needed. That would leave the number in that position yet further diminished.

We could sense that the Germans seemed ready to move in for the kill, because, judging from the sounds, they couldn't have been more than a house or two away. Captain Jordan, fully aware of our predicament, called to us and told us that there was really only one alternative and that was to call fire down on our own position. At this point, those few of us who were there, felt so sure of the impending assault on our position, that we had little trepidation whatsoever about this. At least we knew that we would have some warning about the incoming barrage, giving us time to press into the rubble as hard as we could. Captain Jordan called in the co-ordinates for the fire, and, remarkably, it fell all around us, and not one round fell inside the walls of that foundation. Whatever reservations we might have had about the decision, it seemed to have done the job, because we did have a respite from any immediate action against us.

One of the mysteries of that action that a few of us had wrestled with for years is, who had given the orders to withdraw, because unknown to those of us who were in that position at that time, not only had our Company withdrawn, but also the 75th unit that was behind us. To suggest that there was a mass abandonment of that position that night would be totally false for the simple reason, that there were too many men there who would never leave a position at all unless they were specifically ordered to do so. Someone gave the order. This was not an illustrious night for our unit, but whatever was done, was done at the behest of someone with authority.

At daybreak, the order came to those of us who were there inside the walls of the rubble filled foundation of that house to fall back to a small stone barn that was to the left rear of the position we had been occupying. Again, who issued the order, I do not know, but I would adamantly affirm that there was not one move made on the part of those of us who were there that was not done under command.

Once more we would have to brace ourselves to make a dash through that field of fire, which was laid down by that machine gun firing from our left front. The last few of us who had been in that forward position made the withdrawal without incident or casualty. When we reached the small stone barn, it was already occupied by a handful of men. Out back, behind this barn, was a light machine gun manned by two men; inside, there were several men in place in the hayloft in the top of the barn, and on ground level, the windows were also manned. In total, there couldn't have been more than ten men now in that building. After having been up all night, and not remembering when we had eaten last, I was quite hungry and happened to have a small tin of cheese, the least desirable of all rations, in my pocket. I had just opened this can of cheese, when someone up in the hayloft called down that there was a German tank approaching down a roadway that ran east of the barn. (This would have been to the left of the roadway as we entered the village.)

Soon a second tank was mentioned and then a third; by the fourth, my appetite was completely gone and I discarded the can of cheese. This counting continued until he had numbered thirteen tanks, each one carrying a compliment of Infantry. When this tank column was directly opposite us, one of the men on the light machine gun behind the barn opened up on this column. Several gun turrets swung over in our direction. One fired and with one round there were two dead men beside that weapon, proving that discretion is the better part of valor. As this column of tanks continued on its way, we knew that it would eventually bypass not only us, but would also move by the place where the half-tracks too would be cut off. This is what appeared to us as we witnessed the events in that barn.

As all of this was transpiring, there were some shouted communications between Captain Jordan and the young Lieutenant whom I did not know, but who was now in command of our small detachment in that barn. Precisely what was said, we did not know, but from what we gathered, the Lieutenant must have suggested trying to return to the half-tracks, but Capt. Jordan must have ordered him to stay. The sum of it was that the young officer said that whatever we would do would be decided by those of us in the barn and no one else; most democratic, but a highly unmilitary concept. I must confess, that the only time I ever voted in the Army was in that small barn, and the vote was unanimous to try to make it back to the half-tracks.

With the events unfolding so rapidly, I believe we voted the way we did because of the electrifying effect that the news of the Malmady massacre had on everyone. We had heard that the German units were killing prisoners, and some of our men had also seen some of the Belgian civilians that had been killed by the enemy in the La Gleize area. This, although not once mentioned, contributed most certainly to our decision.

Since the German column was fully in view, we knew that getting out of that barn would not be a simple matter. One by one we made our way out of the barn, past the bodies of those two dead men on that machine gun, through a series of cattle fences, and then up that steep embankment that would bring us onto the elevated roadway. I knew that once we were up on the road there was a ditch on the far side that would offer some protection, but the question was, would the column take notice of this handful of men and do something about it. Fortunately, we must have been considered small prey, because nothing was done to hinder us.

The burden of leaving a place that you have already taken is an immeasurable one, and that feeling, along with the sight that greeted me as I made my way back up that roadway was not only unpleasant, but even sickening. The ditch beside that roadway was littered with all kinds of gear, all of it just about brand new, that had been thrown away as the new troops had hastily retreated.

When I got back to the half-tracks, I was surprised by the almost casual attitude that seemed to prevail there, in such a contrast to the desperate situation that we had just left and the serious threat that seemed to be developing so close at hand.

There were already the brilliantly colored panels displayed on the vehicles for aerial recognition purposes, coinciding with the appearance of several P-38's. I had always considered this aircraft to be the most beautiful and graceful in all of our aerial arsenal, and its appearance was a pleasant surprise. We had heard, however, that some P-38's had caught one of our Companies in the Battalion and mauled it quite severely, so this tempered my feelings somewhat. One aspect of their performance, as they appeared to be working over the German column that was threatening us, was the contrast between the pilots of the P-38's and those of the P-47's. The P-38's came in rather quickly and made dives that were quite shallow in comparison to the P-47's. When the 47's came in for close support, it seemed as though they circled endlessly, but when they came in, they came with long steep dives that seemed to make them most accurate and effective.

By this time I was feeling completely exhausted and so I climbed onto the hood of our half-track to rest, but no sooner had I done this when an irate officer, who I believe was a Colonel, pulled up in a Jeep. He demanded to know what we were doing there and why we were not down in the village. By this time the threatening German column must have been stalled by the air bombardment and eventually retreated. The Colonel told us that he would have the artillery pour smoke and white phosphorous into the village for about twenty minutes and then, without fail, we would take the place.

Within a very few minutes we again were on our way down that roadway, this time in the daylight, moving at a very quickened pace. The whole valley was now shrouded in smoke, giving us some degree of protection. No sooner did we reach the edge of the village, when again we were greeted with heavy machine gun fire. The tanks, along with a few Bazooka rounds eventually silenced some of them, and we moved through quite rapidly. Once again we would have to pass the bodies of Lt. Mellitz and Wertman; the body of one man lay fallen over the hitch of a small trailer that had been abandoned in a previous engagement; the other man was right beside him.

A Brief Respite

When we entered one of the first partially intact houses on the left side of the street, we were met by a Belgian woman who had somehow survived that awful ordeal of fire. Standing in a large room with the floor literally covered from wall to wall with blood, she described a meeting that some of the German soldiers had in that room the night before, in which they were discussing the idea of surrendering. Evidently that counsel must have voted too, in favor of not being taken prisoner. What a haunting bit of information that was. We can only conjecture what would have happened if we had just prevailed a bit longer and more persistently.

After we eliminated some of the machine guns that held up our initial entry into the village, the fire did subside a little, although there were other machine guns that continued to harass us continually. Later in the day we caught a particularly heavy barrage from what must have been that column of tanks that had withdrawn behind the village and then thrown this particularly heavy fire on us.

There was a troublesome sniper who made life rather difficult for us during the course of the night, especially when we were on guard duty by a water trough near the eastern entrance of the town. The next morning, we decided that he must have been in the steeple of the solitary chapel in the village, so we put a Bazooka round through the door of the church, and strangely, the sniper fire ended.

There was a particularly strange incident that occurred in the closing moments of the retaking of the village, when George Sampson and I were moving toward one of the few remaining houses in the village. We approached a side street, and literally bumped into an American coming up that side street, and who was it, but Major McGeorge, armed with nothing but his map case, and a .45. What a remarkable man!

That day we again mounted our half-tracks and headed for a rear area where we located inside a farm compound. This would be our first significant break since being committed in the La Gleize action. Since this was in a relatively well-protected area, our situation could now be much more relaxed, and this permitted us certain liberties that were otherwise unthinkable. The important one was simply to hook up the radio that we had, wiring it to the half-track battery and we could have the enjoyment of listening to music.

After days and nights of that unceasing tension of the combat environment, we entered the kitchen of that Belgian farmhouse, we took off our gear, stacked it along the kitchen wall, slid onto the long wooden benches that surrounded the table, and just sat there wearily looking at each other. Someone had already hooked up the radio and brought it into the house and set it on the table in front of us. The radio was turned to the Armed Forces Network Station, which was broadcast from London. What occurred next sounds so staged and contrived that I was reluctant to include it, but it was neither staged nor contrived, simply one of those inexplicable moments that life constantly produces.

The woman's voice from London then said, "I would like to dedicate this next song to the men of the Third Armored Division. The name of the song is 'I'll Get By.'" The words to that song were, "I'll get by as long as I have you, through there be rain and darkness too, I'll not complain, I'll see it through. Poverty may come to me, it's true, but what care I, say, I'll get by as long as I have you." At this time I was nineteen years old and single, but with me were a number of married men, some with children. The impact of that song at that moment was so emotionally devastating, so charged, that several of those men simply broke down, and without embarrassment, sat and wept.

The Red and White Path: One Soldier's Odyssey

Tiger tank at La Gleize by "December 1944 Museum"

With Mr. Gerard Gregoire, museum curator, author and historian

The gray stone buildings of the small Belgian farm compound provided a cozy haven for half-track D-23 and a tranquil respite for our 3rd Rifle Squad from the 48 nightmarish hours spent in reclaiming the shell-shattered village of Grandmenil. Numbed with that special weariness that sleeplessness and foodlessness inflict on the body, we eyed deliciously those simple amenities that would now make possible a hot meal, sleep without intrusion and time to untangle our senses.

Outwardly, Christmas day slipped unheralded through the towns and villages of the Ardennes, but inwardly many brooding hearts must have lamented the way the day honoring the Prince of Peace had been sullied by the ugliness of war.

In our half-tracks we had sung Christmas carols rather heartily in the cold darkness of that Christmas night, but had we known what lay waiting for us beyond the brow of that hill overlooking Grandmenil, we might have sung with less fervor. But now, all of that was behind us. Ahead of us we knew that at least some of the Christmas spirit would be salvaged by that lavish Christmas dinner that we were sure our company kitchen would make every endeavor to get to us.

Our boudoir that night would be the hayloft of a barn, which we would share with several huge, magnificent Belgian draft horses stabled beneath us. For us, the prospect of sleeping in a bed of hay, just having our weary bodies all but disappear into the gentle arms of that bucolic mattress, would indeed be a luxurious delight.

If we had any hope of casually lolling around to the Armed Forces Radio, stretching and yawning to pass time, they were soon dispelled. After a night's sleep and our belated Christmas meal, we were whisked to an area where we relieved another unit in a defensive position. The position was well protected with roll upon roll of concertina wire (coils of barbed wire that are almost impenetrable). Two men occupied each hole, alternating throughout the night on guard duty.

Morpheus would not be so kind to us this night, since we would be spending it in a hard, cramped foxhole. This tour lasted no more than 48 hours and we returned to the familiar farm compound. Our jaws all dropped in unison when we returned to the hayloft and saw a large, gaping hole in the barn roof directly above where we had slept. Feeling it was better to leave well enough alone, we did not pursue too diligently the matter as to precisely when the shell had struck during our absence.

We spent a few more days in a similar guard role, but this time we were able to fulfill our guard duties with the living room of a nearby house as our quarters. The house was occupied by an elderly couple. The old Belgian gentleman would sit very erectly in his chair from morning to evening, dressed in a military uniform replete with medals, as though he were waiting for the sound of a trumpet to signal his final mustering out so he could then join the ranks of the honored dead.

As those days passed, we were, of course, unaware of the vast preparations that were underway for the mounting of a large offensive that would choke off the German penetration in the "Bulge".

Blood and Snow

January 3rd would inaugurate the red and white path that would lead us south to meet the Third Army near the town of Houffalize. The mingling of the blood and snow would, with all too much frequency, call out in harsh cadence the agonizing toll of the pain and death of the slow, bitterly contested march, made brutal by the frigid winter air.

As the hour for mounting the offensive approached, and orders began filtering down through the echelons, our units all over the area began to stir. There was always a feeling of great excitement and exuberance when our entire Armored Division was on the move. It was the excitement of coming out of that feeling of isolation when each small unit was immersed in its own cauldron of battle and joining the rest of the Division. There was the excitement of recognizing the faces of friends and acquaintances of other of our units in passing vehicles, and the joy of seeing that they were still alive and well. The shouts and greetings that were exchanged in passing turned the entire scene into a jubilant survivors' convention on wheels.

It was also the excitement of the very sensation of power when we witnessed tank after tank and half-track after half-track come spilling out of forests, fields, gardens and villages, then funneling onto the highway in one giant phalanx of steel. It was seeing the half-tracks brimming with Infantry, each half-track with the .50 caliber machine gun in the front on the ring mount like a slender index finger pointing the way for the "track" driver, and the heavy water-cooled .30 caliber machine gun hugging the rear of the half-track as if its sole preoccupation was to guard the rack of bed rolls slung outside beneath it. It was seeing tanks almost rearing on their haunches as they surged forward with a sudden transfusion of power. It was seeing tanks with their hatches open with the tank commander presiding in the open turret looking like some modern day, malformed centaur, dispelling the suspicion of the Infantry that tanks were but monstrous, unthinking steel robots, indifferent to the special vulnerability of the single Infantryman, but were indeed occupied by real flesh and blood creatures such as we were. It was in those moments that the unique spirit of camaraderie seemed to peak, and a strong sense of pride in our unit pervaded everyone in this champion Division that had earned its honors in the bloody hedgerows of Normandy, in its spectacular foray across Northern France and Belgium, and then in crushing the dragon teeth in the mouth of the Siegfried Line.

The roadways were treacherous with ice, the snowy surface having been packed to a glaze by the thousands of tons of vehicles traversing every foot of the highway. Along the way, vehicles that had skidded out of control could be seen at the bottom of embankments in all kinds of awkwardly disabling positions.

No sooner had this massive column reached its crescendo of roaring, clanking, screeching sounds, than units began peeling off to pre-assigned points on what would be the line of departure. Once more we would find ourselves receding into that feeling of isolation, as our small detachment would find itself in some lonely outpost where the point of attack would begin.

When the half-track leaves the roadway and coils with the others in an adjoining field, you know it is now time to go through the perfunctory ritual of checking your gear and making sure that the cartridge belts are full and that there are at least two bandoliers of ammunition crisscrossing your body, along with a couple of grenades to join the K-Rations already stuffed into your pockets.

As you step out of the rear of the half-track, you are always aware of how Divinely gracious the provision is that does not permit you to know what the next day or even the next hour holds in store for you. It would have proven most disconcerting had I known that that step from the rear of the half-track would be the last one taken in a combat role, and that the next twelve days would be one intense, unrelenting span of action with but that triumvirate of fear, cold, and sleeplessness as my clinging companions.

The roads all seemed to look alike, each lined with trees placed at such precise intervals, standing there so rigidly at attention, providing us with that omni-present Ardennes honor guard. The forests behind them, planted with such perfect symmetry, gave the appearance of a vast military host drawn up to witness silently the bloody spectacle about to take place within its ranks.

A Comrade Dies

It was late afternoon before the column of tanks and Infantry finally moved down the roadway to make its initial contact with the enemy. In a very short time we came upon a very substantial roadblock, consisting of a number of large trees that had been felled across the road. The lead squads were instructed to leave the road and move around the roadblock. No sooner had we left the road and moved into some rather thick brush, when we were met with a flurry of rifle fire and several hand grenades exploding in the middle of our small group. There was an immediate exchange of fire. Our Squad Leader, Lester Fickel, was hit, and a man by the name of Joseph Hughes, of Shenandoah, Pa., was shot in the stomach; in addition, there were several other of our men wounded. We were all stunned, when a short time later, we were told that Hughes had died before even reaching the medical half-track.

Darkness came early in the Ardennes during the month of January, so we were told that we would remain in place for the night just where our comrades had fallen. That night I discovered the comfort of crawling under a spruce tree, with its boughs touching the ground, and curling around its trunk and resting on a soft, dry bed of pine needles. For some reason, no one dug in that night.

The action that we had run into that first day ended with some loud and excited shouts from the German soldiers that we had encountered. The voice of the enemy always introduces a more frightening dimension into any exchange, because when there is a voice behind that rifle or behind that thrown grenade, you know that you are not simply the target of some inanimate object, spitting bullets or explosive; you are the target of another mortal being who is really trying to kill you. Hearing the voice of the enemy is certainly not an unusual occurrence in combat situations, but my most memorable instance of this circumstance occurred in our first engagement in the Bulge near the village of La Gleize.

Our squad had been ordered at night to cross a narrow bridge and then leave the roadway, ascend partway up a hill and then follow a course that would parallel the road. As we made our way up the hill, all that we could hear was the snipping of the wire cutter as our squad leader made his way through several cattle fences that obstructed our path. We reached a point, perhaps 50 yards from the road, and then began movement parallel with the roadway, crossing a brook that flowed down off the hill, and then proceeding a few more yards. In the quietness of the night, we heard the unmistakable sound of the bolt of a machine gun being pulled back into a load position. Everyone hit the ground and froze. Then everything ripped loose. The machine gun, which was no more than a very few yards from the forward man in the squad, opened fire. Fortunately for us, the gun must have been set to fire on that narrow bridge that we had just crossed. Had it not been for his discipline in firing into his pre-assigned target, and had he merely turned that gun a few degrees to the left, the gunner would have, without question, made casualties of all of us.

No sooner had the machine gun opened up, than the night was alive with heavy rifle fire and the unmistakable sound of exploding hand grenades all around us. We had walked into a perfect trap. To make the scene complete, there was the pop of flare guns, followed by the eerie light of the flares with the swishing sound as they burned and illuminated the area. We had moved into an L shaped German position, with the machine gun at the end of the short leg of the L. Then from one end of the enemy position to the other, there rang out a chorus of shouts and curses, and demands to surrender in German and halting English, like counter point to the deadly serenade of machine gun and rifle fire, and exploding grenades, played under a canopy of descending flares. Our squad was lying on the ground head to toe, each of us trying frantically to crawl bodily into our steel helmets to escape the blistering torrent of fire.

It was then that the order to pull back was breathlessly and hoarsely whispered along the line. The prospect of getting out of there alive seemed, at the moment, to be just about nil. One of our men became so disoriented that he crawled in the wrong direction and was captured. The rest of us squirmed to a 180-degree turn and then tried to make our way back. I was immediately faced with the prospect of crossing the small brook, which had a cattle fence passing right over it. The lower strand of the wire was too high to get over because of the firing, and too low to get under, but the man behind me became inpatient with my efforts and solved my dilemma by placing his foot firmly on my posterior and literally catapulting me across the brook and through the wire.

As I crawled on my stomach, I passed several motionless forms of men whom I presumed to be dead. After some distance of crawling on my stomach, I was able at least to get up on my hands and knees, and then after some distance more, being beneath the trajectory of fire, I was able to stand up. The machine gun was still pouring fire onto the bridge that we had crossed earlier, so using it was out of the question. It was therefore necessary to wade through the stream that the bridge passed over.

After we returned to a barn, dripping wet, to lick our wounds and count our casualties, George Sampson nervously pulled a cigarette out of his pocket. When he reached for his lighter, he was shocked because he didn't recognize it. Instead of the dull, tarnished lighter that he was used to, he pulled out a lighter that was glistening. The friction from crawling on his stomach had cleaned it so thoroughly that it gleamed beyond recognition.

In spite of all that had happened that night, it was always the sound of the shouts, the jeering and the cursing in German, the voice of the enemy, that made the deepest and the most searing impression on my memory.

Self-preservation Instinct

After spending the night under the spruce tree, interrupted only for periods of guard duty, when daylight came, the roadblock that was encountered the night before was quickly removed. No sooner had that obstacle been overcome than we were faced with a blown-out bridge that required another delay to permit the engineers to replace it. It was those delays that were always so maddening; the inactivity in the numbing cold added so much more to our physical discomfort. It was at such times that if at all possible we would try to steal a few moments to huddle behind the rear of the tank to capture some of the heat from the exhaust of the engine.

Tank columns must have been at the very top of the priority list for the German forward artillery observers, for the shelling of the column was constant. The delays to permit our own artillery to demolish and soften up some strong point, or the delays to permit the lead tank element to work over some stubborn defensive position always made the Infantry so much more vulnerable to the incoming fire from the German artillery. This produced a love-hate relationship between tanks and Infantry. We loved them when we ran into heavy small arms and machine gun fire because of their effectiveness in overcoming that type of resistance, but we hated them because of the heavy fire they brought upon themselves and us. At night when all was quiet, the sound of the tank generator starting up and running would further incense us because we knew it would just invite more trouble. So it must ever be that the instinct of self-preservation will always produce its overriding prejudices.

Hob-nail Boots v. Galoshes

Later, in that same day, we approached one of those small, nameless hamlets with its houses clustered around a very sharp horseshoe bend in the road. Just before the first houses there was a road that let off to the right at a perpendicular to the road on which we were moving. The Infantry immediately began clearing the houses. No sooner had some of us entered the houses, when a machine gun opened up behind us and began pouring heavy fire down that side road, cutting the lead elements from those following. Those of us who had entered the houses must have interrupted the preparation of the evening meal because there was some food on the stoves. I grabbed a small pan of hot milk and gulped it down. It was delicious.

The firing at the intersection behind us was still rather furious. I ran across the street to the solitary house located in the very center of this horseshoe turn. As I ran up the pavement to the entrance of the house, the door flew open and two German soldiers came bursting out, almost into my arms. Fortuitously, at that moment, the lead tank came easing around the corner and they threw their hands into the air. Passing off prisoners to the rear was never much of a problem because it seemed there were always a few men who made a career out of taking the prisoners back, having discovered the luxury of absenting themselves from the deadly, continuing drudgery of the forward elements.

On this occasion, as I began moving these two prisoners toward the street, I encountered a lieutenant. I asked him what I should do with them and he simply replied, "Take them back to Battalion yourself ". I was pretty certain that if it hadn't been for the machine gun fire that was still holding up matters at the intersection, I would not have been the one taking them back. I indicated to the two prisoners that they should start moving back up the road. By this time it was just starting to get dark, and there was still some sporadic firing at the intersection, so I indicated to the two of them as dramatically as possible that they should start to run. And run we did. We made it through the intersection without incident and continued past the remainder of our column as it was paused on the road. I had no idea where Battalion Headquarters was, and by now we were on a very lonely road still going at top speed because I didn't know how to tell them to slow down.

When I had taken them prisoner, I had immediately removed all their gear from them, helmets, and of course weapons, and other military gear, so that they were stripped of all unnecessary weight. However, they still did retain their hob-nailed boots, which made excellent heavy-duty track shoes. I, on the other hand, had all my gear, with all its clumsy bulk, and for foot wear, nothing but a classic old pair of galoshes, which were like racing slicks on a surface that was mirror smooth because of the passing tanks. The inevitable happened, and I went sprawling, sending my helmet bouncing along the icy surface of the road. The prisoners immediately halted in their tracks. It was a very tense moment on that deserted roadway, since I did not know what the prisoners' response would be. Fortunately, my rifle had remained firmly in my grasp.

Crawling on my hands and knees, I recovered my helmet, put it in place, and then got up. I nodded to the two of them to proceed, and proceed they did, immediately breaking into a run again. Finally, I saw a house in the distance with a number of Jeeps clustered around it, and was happy to know that I had found Battalion Headquarters. I met a GI who was willing to accept the prisoners, so I was finally able to divest myself of my two track stars. My return to the squad was made with a little less duress. That night we spent at a small barn at the edge of the hamlet, alternately sleeping inside and pulling guard outside.

A Few Yards a Day

Our artillery spent most of the night shelling the village directly
ahead of us, and the evidence as we approached it the next
morning, was unmistakable. They had done a thorough job. The
great devastation of all of those shelled villages was so similar;
trees shorn of branches that littered the ground beneath them as
though some giant pruning shears had gone amok; walls of houses
with the curtains fluttering through holes where windows once had
been; broken power lines drooping from poles, snaking their way
through the snow to nowhere; piles of rubble with hot embers from
burnt beams underneath, steaming holes through the covering of
freshly fallen snow. Heartbreaking desolation.

Constantly pushing forward was gruelingly slow and humanly very
costly. But one of the ironies of combat is that you are actually in
touch with so few people, that you are sometimes unaware of the
extent of the human cost. You are aware of what is happening to
your squad and possibly one or two other squads, but aside from
that you are almost totally oblivious as to what is going on around
you, even across the street from you. The medical half-track might
be busy evacuating people who have been wounded and possibly
even killed in one of the other platoons, and you might be
completely unaware of it. That is why combat experience has such
a narrow focus.

It was obvious that our day's objective would be the high ground
ahead of us. As we wended our way towards the crest, the column
was suddenly enveloped in a fierce and sustained barrage of
artillery fire. For the Infantry, there was nowhere to take shelter, no
ditches or depressed areas in which to escape the intensity of the
fire. Simultaneously, George Sampson, Harry Clark and I, without
a word, decided on the same course of action. There was a small
wooded area about 150 yards off to the right of the roadway, and
we decided to make a run for it and wait out the barrage in
whatever shelter the woods might provide. Inspired by the volume
and the devastating accuracy of the incoming fire, we moved at a

rapid pace across the snowy field. As we burst through the first fringe of trees, we were astonished to be met, in a well dug-in position, by a half dozen German soldiers with their arms raised. Years later they probably regaled their grandchildren as to how they were captured when their position was overrun in a fearless charge by three American soldiers.

As dusk approached, the crest had still not been attained. At that point, we were ordered to mount the tanks. The final several hundred yards would be made with the tanks moving abreast up the snowy slope. As the attack began, tracers arched out from the front of every tank, converged on a tree line on the top of the hill, and then disappeared as their trajectories were exhausted. As the tanks moved the final few yards to the tree line, there were several explosions as a few of the tanks struck mines covered by the freshly fallen snow.

After we dismounted from the tanks, we were told that we would be spending the night along the tree line. I had decided that I did not intend to do any digging that night. I planned instead to spend the night under one of the tanks that had been disabled after striking a mine. This tank was located only about 30 feet off to the left of the roadway leading to the next village.

Although the tank was disabled, it was, nevertheless, still occupied by the crew. The tankers were always very generous with us, so there was no problem when I asked if they could spare some blankets. They gave me a hefty supply, which at least boded well for a reasonably comfortable night. I shared my plans with Fred Dorsey. He liked the idea and decided to join me.

After we had been there a short while, a Jeep came up to us bringing rations and water for our unit. There was a lot of slipping and tripping and falling in the snow as the rations were distributed among the men.

When the guard roster was made up, it was decided that a tree located on the far side of the roadway would be the primary guard post. Our time on guard would be from 2 to 4.

Dorsey and I spread our blankets under the rear of the tank, and what with the extravagant number of blankets and some residual heat from the tank engine, we were quite comfortable. But it seemed in no time at all we were awakened for our tour of guard duty. After we crawled out from under the tank, Dorsey told me that under no circumstances would he agree to go over to the other side of that roadway to the tree to pull guard. I argued with him that we had no choice, since it was the assigned position. He remained adamant, and foolishly I relented and agreed to pull guard by the tank, but I did insist that we move forward of the tank. Dorsey agreed, and with the luminous-dialed guard watch, having been handed to us, we began that two-hour guard tour.

Two hours of standing in numbing cold, trying to be as alert as possible is a challenging ordeal. Chewing on fruit bars or the hard chocolate bars helped to occupy the time and bring a small bit of heat and energy. Foot stamping is always good for short intervals, as long as it doesn't interfere with the listening. One of the essential rituals of guard duty is always to urinate. This becomes such an unvarying part of guard procedure that weeks later when I was hospitalized, invariably every night's sleep would be interrupted because of this self-induced call developed so rigidly during guard duty. Our guard tour did end after that always seemingly interminable two-hour stint. George Sampson and the man he had dug in with that night were to relieve us, so I went to their hole, wakened them, and gave them the guard watch. As soon as they made their way to the tree across the road to begin their guard tour, Dorsey and I crawled between our blankets underneath the tank.

We had just fallen asleep when we were awakened by a commotion behind us. Because of the unusual nature of the disturbance, we crawled out to investigate, and saw Sampson and the other soldier with several German prisoners. It happened that a very short time after they had assumed their guard position, a German patrol had stealthily made its way up the ditch on the far side of the road and was intercepted by George and his companion. This had a very shattering effect on me because I had not insisted on being at the guard position where we were supposed to be. When I realized the implications of what could have happened if that patrol had come a few minutes earlier and gotten behind us, the damage that could have been inflicted because of our negligence, I was overtaken with a real sense of shame at my dereliction of one of the most elementary responsibilities of a soldier.

What made it sting all the more was the memory of an experience when I was involved in a defensive position in the Stolberg area. There had been several holes grouped together in a woods, and the hole in the center of the group was to be the primary guard post. Two at a time, during the night, we would move to that hole and the guard watch would be passed to those on duty. On one occasion, John Eumurian and I, who had dug in together, crawled out of our foxhole one morning, and only a few feet away from our hole was a new, freshly oiled ammunition clip to a German Machine-Pistol. Someone had been negligent on guard duty. A German patrol had been permitted to pass only a few feet from us and could have caused deadly havoc in our ranks. I remembered how angry I was then, and now that I might have been the culprit in a similar situation, I was deeply shaken.

As daylight came, a Jeep came up the road. As it neared us, there was a loud explosion as the Jeep hit a mine. The two men in the Jeep were seriously injured, and within a very short time, men with mine detectors were brought up. Mine after mine was picked up throughout the area where we were located. It was the Teller mines, strewn hastily under the freshly fallen snow that people had been slipping and stumbling over the night before while distributing rations. The crowning moment came, however, when a Teller mine was removed from directly underneath the rear of the tank where Dorsey and I had slept. The knowledge that you spent the night sleeping on a Teller mine is frightening.

The delay in clearing the area of mines was considerable, so it was quite late till the column began to move once more. Ahead of us down the slope was the village of Regny. Again, the artillery had done its work and the village was literally in shambles. Nevertheless, the platoon ahead of us met stubborn resistance and progress was exceptionally slow. Daylight hours were very short and it always seemed that we were bumping into darkness. By the time we moved through the village and a short distance beyond, daylight was failing, and a very heavy snowstorm had developed. There were isolated houses scattered along the roadway, and we had taken one of the houses on the left side of the road, hoping that we would be remaining there for the night. The usual formality of blacking out the windows with whatever material was at hand was immediately taken care of.

Blizzards and the Blues

Shortly after this was done, Pop Waters, our Platoon Sgt., came in and said he needed a few volunteers for something that needed to be done; nothing of a particularly hazardous nature. Since I was standing by him and didn't volunteer, he gave me a particularly sharp dressing down. My spirits were already low because of the guard incident the night before, and now this rebuke on top of that pushed my spirits down another couple of notches because I had great admiration for Pop Waters.

Sometime later, after we were pretty comfortably situated, Pop Waters again returned and said that the 3rd Rifle Squad should get geared up and ready to move out. It was reported that a German tank was roaming around up on some high ground on the other side of the road and they wanted the Bazooka team up there to guard our flank.

By this time, the snow was falling and the wind blowing in blizzard proportions. We made our way through ever deepening snow to the high ground where we were to dig in for the night. When we arrived at the top I took off my gear and stacked it against a tree in preparation to digging in. I just stood there and was overtaken with a dark, brooding feeling of despair; in the bitter cold, with the wind screaming through the naked branches of the trees, now being driven so fiercely that it stung my face like hundreds of pin pricks.

The prospect of spending hours chiseling through the frozen crust of earth and then shivering till daylight, languishing in that frozen pit with the sound of a marauding German tank in the distance, along with the several dispiriting events that occurred during the last 24 hours, sent my spirits plummeting. Standing there, I contemplated the futility of it all; to go through all of this, and then possibly as a final recompense to have my crumpled body found lifeless in the snow and heaved ignominiously onto the back of a three-quarter ton truck brought me to the point of almost total despair. As I stood there like a spectator to my own misery, the bleakness of that wintry hill reflected accurately the bleakness of my own spirit.

In God's Hands

Village of Hebronval

With Jose Burnotte

Nevertheless, I joined George and we selected a spot and scooted the snow away and started to dig. After digging for some time, someone called our attention to a figure that could be seen making its way up the path that we had taken, approaching through the heavy falling snow. It was one of our men. As he approached, he shouted that he had a message for us. We were to return down to the Company because orders had come down from Regiment that all troops were to be in shelter. The toll taken by the weather was almost exceeding that taken by the enemy. It didn't take us long to gather our things together and begin to make our way down to the rest of the Company.

This time we didn't return to the same house that we had left previously. We were directed to another house, which was already occupied, and fortunately, by the time we arrived, the men had already made up their guard roster, so we were excluded. This gave us time to rest up and thaw out from that long hilltop excursion.

The next morning, as we prepared to move out, an additional snow accumulation of 10 to 12 inches greeted us, but at least the snowstorm had ended.

As we approached the next village, there was by the side of the road, a yellow sign edged with a curtain of driven snow and the name Hebronval visible through it. One of the first buildings to be entered was a shed-type building attached to a house. Harry Clark entered it and had an old fashioned shoot out with a German soldier and finished him.

At this point, the tanks refused to move any farther for reasons that we were unaware of at the time. While everything was stalled, the Infantry took up positions along the roadside among some of the scattered buildings. On the left side of the roadway, I took my position by a small wood shed. As I stood guard there, I was deeply concerned and appalled at the horribly despondent frame of mind into which I had slipped during the last 48 hours. It was an attitude that was absolutely deadly, since I knew it was stealing away the alertness and the initiative that were so essential if one was to at least attempt to survive. I prayed a desperate prayer for help, an inarticulate cry for Divine intervention. What soldier would not want to have complete assurance that he would survive the ordeal of war, but to have that assurance was not my lot. There was a response; however, it seemed to be simply "All is well. All is well." Although I still did not have the assurance that I would not die, I knew my days were in God's hands. As a consequence, I experienced a quieting of the spirit and even a feeling of buoyancy that would not desert me.

With the quieting of my spirit, my senses were again attuned to our immediate situation. We could hear the muffled radio communications from inside the tanks, with the static and constant interruptions in tones of urgency. Someone then told us that the reason the tanks were not moving was because they feared mines. After encountering that minefield on the hill two nights before, they feared that the Germans might have again taken advantage of the freshly fallen snow and strewn a hasty minefield.

Friends and Foes

Someone asked for two volunteers to walk in front of each track of the lead tank, shuffling the snow to locate mines that might have been lying immediately under the freshly fallen snow. Harry Clark and I volunteered to do this and got the column moving. Shuffling the deep snow was particularly laborious and painstakingly slow.

As we moved farther into the village, we approached a curve in the road, and poised right on the curve was a solitary house with the windows already shattered. It looked especially menacing because of its location. The situation of the house was perfect for a Panzerfaust team (a German Bazooka team) with covering riflemen. Harry and I began firing into the openings of the house. With the roar of the tank engine immediately behind us, in addition to our preoccupation with the possibility of mines, a rifle shot from that distance ahead of us would have been impossible to hear. There are often parallel circumstances that quickly excite latent fears and conjure up unpleasant memories that prompt instinctive responses. Over all of the noise we heard the voice of a corporal behind the lead tank shouting at us to quit firing, because he said there might be some Germans in there, who might want to surrender. Harry and I replied to him that we would gladly stop firing if he would exchange places with us in front of the tank. With that we heard no more from him.

The firing that Harry and I did was not a wanton or trigger-happy escapade, but a justified response to what was perceived to be a real threat despite the cries of that feckless protestor sheltered behind the lead tank.

By this time the tanks had moved far enough without incident to assure the tankers that the possibility of mines was no longer there. Harry and I broke away and joined the others in moving through and clearing houses.

There was a road that cut off to the left of the main street leading to a Chapel and another part of the village. Those men who entered the Chapel, among them, George Sampson and Harry Clark, found the body of a young girl in the front of the sanctuary, laid out in preparation for burial. I had joined up with Charles Craig and proceeded up the main street with several other men, working through the houses on either side of the street.

One of the first houses I entered, I had entered alone. As I ran through it, I bumped into a German soldier in the doorway between two rooms. He immediately raised his arms in surrender, and then gestured that he wanted to get something from his pocket. He reached into his pocket and pulled out a small change purse, and from it he retrieved some kind of skiing medal. It must have been something he valued because he offered it to me, and then thrust the purse into my hand in a further attempt to ingratiate himself to his captor. I felt quite sure that if we had been together a few more minutes, we could have been good friends. I ushered him to the door and indicated to him that he should move down the street to the rear with his hands clasped behind his head.

I joined Craig and we entered another house. Craig was armed with nothing but a Walkie-Talkie and the Army .45 automatic. The .45 was a weapon that I'm sure most men would have been more effective in throwing than in shooting. Nevertheless, Craig seemed to feel adequately secure carrying that piece of equipment. One house, which we entered together, found Craig immediately rushing upstairs to check it out, while I went to the rear of the house on the first floor. In the rear of the house was a room with an open stairway leading to the cellar. There was just a railing around the open stairway and the steps leading to the cellar were very steep. At the bottom of the stairs was a door, but it was located in such a fashion that it would have been extremely difficult to open and at the same time have the rifle in a ready position.

The prospect of going down those steps did not appeal to me at all, so I shouted down, "Kommen sie raus mit den handen hoche!" I shouted this twice, without any response. I then began to leave, but as I approached the front door and saw that Craig had already left,

I became apprehensive, because once you leave a house, the others following have every right to believe it has been cleared. I returned to the rear of the house again to the stairway and shouted down again. "Kommen sie raus mit den handen hoche!" Still, no response, and I was still determined not to go down those steps. I didn't like the idea of using hand grenades because of the possibility of civilians taking refuge there. Standing in the corner at the top of the stairway was a wooden hay rake. I picked it up and threw it with as much force as I could. It bounced down the steps with an awful racket, slammed into the door, and instantly, the door burst open and four German soldiers come hurriedly through it and up the steps with their hands raised, all chanting the prisoners chorus, "Comrade!" "Comrade!" "Comrade!"

The houses on the street where we were working were finally cleared and four of us found ourselves by a small outbuilding at the edge of the village, waiting for orders as to what we should do next. Craig, meantime, had been summoned and had returned back down the street. In a very short time Pop Waters approached us and told us that the Company was going to change directions and would be moving out of the village on another road. However, he said to me, "Take these guys and go down the road and clear those two houses." My heart sank, because those two houses were about a quarter of a mile away and the long open roadway was nothing but an unending series of undulating snow drifts. The snow had drifted in depths that ranged from knee to navel deep. We moved out again with the wearying chore of breaking snow, burdened with all that equipment, particularly that necessary nuisance, the entrenching tool, banging you in the backside with every step you took. With snow at such depths, we did not walk through the snow; we climbed through it.

As we approached the halfway mark, tensions began mounting considerable, knowing that we must make outstanding targets in our dark uniforms against the brilliantly white snow.

Moving closer to the objective, we could see that the house-barn combination on the right side of the road was nearer, but the squat house on the left looked more ominous. I felt that if there were trouble, it would issue from that house. After that long struggle over completely open terrain, all I wanted was shelter, so when we got reasonably close, I decided to make a run for the nearer house on the right side of the road, so that we could at least get inside and catch our breath before we made our move on the other house. I dashed up the step and crashed against the front door, bouncing off! It was locked!

There was now nothing else to do but make the final dash for the other house. With the other guys in my tracks and, I imagine, each one holding his breath, we rushed diagonally across the street. I pushed in the front door into a medium sized room. When my eyesight recovered from the blinding snow, I found myself in the midst of at least twelve German soldiers. Some were standing, others seated, and all of them were surrounded with a frightening array of weaponry, and yet, realizing it was all nullified because they had made a decision to surrender. When I realized what damage they could have inflicted, in view of their commanding position and deadly amount of weaponry, my emotions veritably ricocheted back and forth between terror and euphoria. To have such tension broken with such elation must have carried us away, because Pop Waters, evidently wondering where we were, had followed us to see what was taking so long. Although his actions demonstrated his concern, his appearance was as though he knew that all we had to do was to hike through the snow, pick up some prisoners and return. At least there was one real tangible reward from that incident, because one of the prisoners "agreed" to give me a beautifully holstered Spanish .38 that he was carrying.
That unusual day at Hebronval was a day I desperately needed. There wasn't a day like it before or after. That day seemed to be the Divinely orchestrated response to the prayerful interlude by the woodshed earlier in the day, at the entrance to the village.

Callous Killing

Our unit now changed direction and moved out of Hebronval in a southerly direction toward high ground ahead of us, and after moving some distance in a tank and Infantry column, there was a short, but heavy, exchange of fire as we approached a small wooded area. As we moved through it, we came upon two badly wounded German soldiers, blood covered and groaning pitifully. The officer with the several of us who stood by them said we should prepare immediately to remove them to the rear. No sooner had he uttered those words, when a man standing by us fired a few rounds from his Thompson sub-machine gun into them, killing them both instantly. We stood there absolutely dumbfounded at this senseless and cowardly action. Ironically, the man who did it was the same man who earlier in the day, yelled at Clark and me for firing into that house because he said, "There might be Germans in there who want to surrender."

There was a rather steep hill between us and our next village objective. It was decided to split the column and have the tanks approach the village around the right side of the hill, while the Infantry would make its way around the left side of the hill.

As this move proceeded, the height of the hill made it impossible to maintain radio contact with the tank column, and there was fear that a lot of dangerous mischief would follow if neither column knew where the other was. An officer ordered Clark and me to make our way to the top of the hill so that we might locate the tank column and so make a coordinated attack on the village possible. Harry and I made our way through the deep snow and finally made it to the crest just about completely exhausted. We spotted our tank column. The tank column spotted us and thought we were Germans, the Germans in the village spotted us and knew we were Americans, and everyone began firing. We burrowed into the snow for a few moments to catch our breath; then we literally threw ourselves down that hill, running, sliding, tumbling, just to get out of there. After the firing, we didn't have to tell the officer where the tank column was. They had decisively reported their location.

The two columns met at the edge of the village, and the tanks laid down heavy fire as we moved into it. Some of our men came upon an elderly Belgian farmer who seemed oblivious to everything that was going on around him because his barn was on fire. After the village was secured, these same men returned and helped him save his barn.

Battle-hardened Men

By the time the village was secured, darkness had already set in. A search was immediately begun for inhabitable quarters since most of the houses had been severely damaged. Several men from our platoon found one where at least the rear of the house was only slightly damaged, although the front of the building had been blown open. It was always amazing how quickly a room could be blacked out so that we could have light as soon as possible. A mattress was dragged from an upstairs bed, and then a large dresser was used to keep the mattress in place in front of the lone window in the room.

Guards were immediately set out while the rest of us prepared enthusiastically for our first warm meal in days. Pop Waters had been carrying with him a tin of sardines that he had received from home. I was fortunate enough to be asked to share this gourmet meal with him.

Things looked pretty good for a reasonable night, in spite of the intermittent shelling. Soon, however, a full-scale artillery barrage came slamming into the village. One shell must have landed at the base of the wall of the house, directly beneath the solitary window. The force of the explosion blew the mattress and the dresser back across the room. We threw ourselves on the candles in order to extinguish the light so as not to jeopardize our position. Just as quickly, the mattress and dresser were again positioned against the window, the candles were located and lighted, and food that hadn't been spilled was recovered and the meal resumed.

A new officer had just joined us that day, and he had been seated on the floor eating when the shell struck our house. Sometime later he said "I can't believe what I've just seen." He continued, asking, "What kind of men are you?" We really didn't know what he was talking about. Then he went on. "When I was in England, if a Buzz Bomb just flew over the camp, everyone would be up all night, no one would sleep. Here, a shell almost lands in the room and you guys act as though nothing happened." There was no response to his observation, because I guess everyone knew he could find the answer for himself soon enough.

A runner came for Pop Waters and told him to report to the Company CP. In a very short time he returned with news we did not want to hear. Our 3rd Rifle Squad was ordered to get its gear together, and we were taken to the edge of the village and ordered to dig in. Sampson and I, with the Bazooka, were ordered to dig in right beside the road, Clark and another man, a few yards from us, and the other team, beyond them. After hacking through the frozen surface, in a very short time, George and I realized that we had inherited a rock quarry. We chiseled and chipped and sweated even in the intense cold, and after hours of this highly unproductive labor, we managed to carve out what must have appeared like nothing more than an oversized, built-in birdbath. A few yards away from us, Harry and his companion must have struck a mother lode of topsoil, because in a very short time, he, as well as the other team, was ensconced in deep, relatively comfortable holes.

Clark managed to pilfer a door from a nearby shed and threw that over the top of their hole for additional warmth and comfort. When we initially were brought to this position, we were told that anything that comes up that road is German. After we had been suffering there a number of hours, we heard the sound of a vehicle approaching us. As it came nearer and nearer, we got into a heated argument as to whether the sound of the oncoming vehicle was actually German. Our argument was more with ourselves than with each other, because as the vehicle approached, we were certain that the sound was decidedly that of an American engine, despite what had been originally told us.

Finally as the vehicle came by us, we were greeted by a cheery American voice. It was the voice of the commander of an American tank destroyer. That man would never know what kind of hell he put us through and how close he came to having a Bazooka round through the side of his vehicle.

Daylight did not come too soon, after that night of cold and suspense. We were finally recalled and joined the rest of the unit. As we re-entered the village we came under exceptionally heavy artillery fire. We took shelter in a shed where a number of our wounded were waiting to be evacuated to the rear. The wounds of some of the men were distressingly bad, and it was doubtful whether evacuation would come in time.

The entire day was again spent in slow forward movement, with the usual pauses for our own artillery to do its work, or standing by while the tanks demolished or silenced some strong point. The incoming fire never really ceased for any length of time, taking its emotional as well as its physical toll. Although the sameness of the nights, the sameness of the landscape, the hunger, the cold, all conspired to dull the senses, it seemed that the one sense to escape this dulling effect was the fear, which, whether mentioned or unmentioned, dogged every step and hovered over every moment. By dusk, we had again reached the next village, with the Germans withdrawing just ahead of us. There were not very many houses in what would be more accurately described as a hamlet rather than a village. The stream that flowed by this small grouping of houses now had to be bridged before we could proceed further. The combat engineers would have the unenviable task of spending the night putting a bridge across the stream under heavy and persistent fire.

Kitchen Sinks and Combat Boots

Troops were continuing to move into the hamlet, taxing the possible places of shelter to the limit. I entered one house that was already just about filled to capacity, with most everybody just milling around. The room I had entered was the kitchen of the house and I spied a kitchen sink that was rather low to the floor, but I could see that there was adequate room underneath for a person to stretch out. I removed my gear and got down and wiggled my way underneath the sink. For me, the physical requirements for a night's rest were absolutely minimal, especially in view of the sleepless night Sampson and I had spent the night before. Neither the view nor the smell, from my vantage point, was very inspiring, what with the dank odor of the sink drain above me and the sight and smell of vintage combat boots in front of me. Nevertheless, I thought I had done really well with the spot I had chosen.

Sometime later, some loud mouth broke the spell of my repose by complaining about the number of men in the building, and began checking into the company affiliation of each man. I concluded from what I heard, that he did not want D Company personnel there, because all except those of another company were being ordered out. I tried to remain indifferent to the proceedings, feeling my benign presence under the sink was harming no one. But I knew my position had been compromised when I saw a large, ungainly combat boot, with flesh overflowing its top, begin probing around under the sink until he finally encountered my body. He was evidently unable to bend over to see me, because he simply kept jabbing at me with his foot until I was forced to respond. I asked him what he wanted. "What's your name soldier?" "Kauffman!" "What company?" "D" "Then get out of here!"

It is one thing to be evicted from some palatial suite, but to be unceremoniously booted out from under a kitchen sink has no insulting or demeaning equal. I struggled out from under the sink, dragging my gear with me and stood to face my antagonist. This humiliation had made me altogether furious, and even though I faced a creature with an arm just burdened with stripes, I told him that I was not a member of some alien unit, but I too was an American soldier and I couldn't see what harm my presence could bring. The exchange became very heated, and after I had words like "insubordination" and "Court-marshal" rifled past me, I realized that the solitary stripe on my arm did not very well buttress my position, so I made a retreat. I opened the door and just before I left, I discharged a barrage of epithets that I was sure would cover all of his human frailties, slammed the door and went sulking out into the darkness looking for a more friendly refuge.

Just a short distance away was a barn, and upon entering it I found it to be just as crowded as the place I had just left. There were in it soldiers, civilians, and a number of dairy cows. For some reason, the cows had been given a very generous allotment of space. Most of the cows were lying down, so I dropped down beside the first one, rested my back against it and found complete comfort. As an added bonus, I was a benefactor of the heat that the animal was generating. After my last ordeal, I decided that I had now found a true Shangri la. The calmness of the animals as they placidly chewed their cud had a particularly tranquilizing effect.

Sometime later there was activity in the opposite corner of the barn. Through the language barrier, I learned that a woman was having a baby. What a time and place, I thought, with local strangers, foreign strangers, and then as if to add final insult, the animals themselves. Yet as I reflected on it, despite the embarrassment of the moment, I wondered if in time to come, the woman might not be overcome with a great sense of pride as she remembered another mother who also gave birth to a Son under similar circumstances, a Son whose first gulp of air on this earth was also the stale air of a stable laden with the smell of manure.

Walking and Wandering

Sometime later, a soldier came to the door of the barn and told us that a barn just a short distance away had been hit by a shell and a number of our soldiers had been killed. I never knew why we always felt so secure in a barn, since in most parts of a barn the only protection was a thin slate or tile roof. The news made me very uneasy, so I decided to leave and find other quarters. Down the street was another house, and as I entered, I found it occupied mostly by men of our company. But again, it was a cellar kitchen that was altogether crowded, with men sitting and standing. I did find a place at a table, but the prospect of sitting up all night in a room that was blue with smoke did not appeal to me, so I moved on again. The kitchen opened directly into a barn that was completely empty except for the dairy cows. Barn or no barn, I wanted a night's rest, so I took off my gear and lay down in a concrete feed trough and finally, after a night of wandering, found a place of rest.

The next day would be a repetition of the preceding days with its drudgery, its hardships, and the disappearance of friends from our ranks, whether by the medical half-track or the ultimate route; that notorious three-quarter-ton truck. We received word that one of our other units had been ambushed and had taken a heavy toll of casualties. The road down which we were moving was in the same direction as that which the hard-hit unit had taken. We were ordered to halt in an area of open, scrubby terrain. Waters come to us and told us that Sampson and I were to move with the Bazooka to a position quite a distance forward of the company and prepare to intercept any tanks that might come down the roadway. We waited for what seemed hours and finally Harry Clark came to us and told us that the company had moved out some time ago in another direction, but somehow they had neglected to tell us. This would not be the last time that Harry would come to our rescue.

We took a very circuitous route, and after walking quite some distance we finally entered a wooded area. Just inside the woods we found a trail and followed it. This path paralleled the edge of the woods, and as we moved forward, some of our men caught a glimpse of several German soldiers darting through the woods ahead of us.

There was at least one other squad ahead of us as we moved single file through the woods. The column came to a halt, and then we could see heads turning as if a message were being passed from one to another. Unfortunately, the message ended with us; the call was for the Bazooka team to make its way forward. Sampson and I made our way forward past the other troops crouched along the pathway. When we arrived at the head of the column, we were told that there appeared to be an enemy vehicle about 100 yards ahead, just inside the woods. The column stayed in place while George and I made our way forward. As we drew nearer, it appeared that the vehicle, which was an armored vehicle, seemed to have been abandoned. But close by was a rather large log bunker, the type which the Germans seemed especially adept at building.

As we moved closer, a German medic appeared at the door wearing a Red Cross vest, and waving a white flag. We then moved rapidly forward and found that the medic spoke rather good English. He told us that there were a number of fellow soldiers inside the bunker and they too wanted to surrender. We told him to tell them to come out with their hands raised, and then to form them in a column of two's to expedite moving them to the rear. At this point, we were no more than 30 or 40 feet inside of the woods. As we formed them up, we heard the sound of tanks and were relieved to see two of our Sherman tanks come sweeping across the open field toward us. We did not realize that what they would see would be a German vehicle, a bunker, and a group of German soldiers.

Terror Under Fire

As they approached, they immediately opened fire and closed into the very edge of the woods. All of us hit the ground. It was a moment of absolute terror. The one tank, to which I was the closest, raked the area back and forth, the coaxial machine gun in the turret sweeping over us again and again. Then at regular intervals a round of high explosive was fired through the trees and into the bunker. George was hanging on bodily to one German soldier who was trying to get away. The audible prayers of the Germans around me, the maddening feeling of helplessness in being fired upon by our own men, it was a total nightmare.

The firing would cease, and we would think that it was all over, but then, whether they spotted movement or for whatever reason, the firing would begin again, the machine guns sweeping over us and the 76's cutting loose and bringing down branches with snow on top of us. We could hear the empty casings of the high explosive rounds clanging on the floor of the tank.

When this whole unfortunate incident began, Harry Clark left his position where we had left the company, made his way out of the woods into the clearing, approached the tanks from the rear, and somehow got their attention and shouted to them that there were American soldiers in that group. The tanks finally quit firing.

Clark and the others stated later that they never expected to see anyone rise up out of the horror alive, and yet every one of us did. There was not one casualty. The only conclusion that we could ever arrive at, aside from Providential intervention, was that the tanks were too close.

After we all collected ourselves, the German medic came at George and me and was absolutely furious because we had let the incident happen. Why he ever thought that we had invited something as horrible as that upon ourselves we will never know, but the circumstances were so unreasonable that anything was forgivable.

By this time the entire column arrived where we were and we again moved out. We came to a small stream where we all replenished our water supply, filling our canteens. Our orders were then to follow the stream. We came to a tributary, and this brought Clark and Sampson into a heated argument, because Sampson would have followed the tributary instead of the main stream. At this point Clark gave a rather lengthy dissertation on the simplicity of determining which is the main stream and which is the tributary. Clark, the classic country boy, the experienced coon hunter, lamented as to how little city boys knew about the out-of-doors.

The going was extremely tough as we made our way up the steep, wooded slope and through the heavy snow. We finally arrived at the top and then moved some distance down the forward slope, the military crest. By this time it was dark and we were told to prepare to dig in. Sampson and I were assigned to dig in directly beside a narrow road that cut through the woods. The digging, again, was extremely difficult. A conspiracy of rocks and roots made the progress painfully slow. The hole we ended up with was adequate, but not at all ideal.

Frozen Overcoats

We placed our raincoats, which we carried folded over the back of our cartridge belts, in the bottom of the hole, for some protection from the cold earth. Sampson was wearing a mackinaw, not the traditional long overcoat that most of us wore. The night was probably one of the coldest that we had thus far encountered, so when we crawled into the hole, I removed my overcoat and covered the both of us with that. It was brutally cold that night and so we slept very little. Sampson spent some time huddled under the overcoat reading his New Testament by the light of his flashlight. We had no interruptions during the night, but we heard later that a German contingent had moved through behind us and captured some of our men, and then later, this same group was, in turn, captured by others of our company. To this, George and I were completely oblivious.

At daybreak, we decided it was pointless to lie in the hole shivering any longer, so we roused ourselves and climbed out to do some foot stamping. The overcoat with which we had covered ourselves was frozen hard as a board from having been wet the previous day. I literally had to break the arms of the coat and the other surfaces to make the coat pliable enough so that I could put it on. While I was doing that, I had propped my rifle against a nearby tree. George, meanwhile, had spotted a German patrol coming up the ditch toward us on the same side of the roadway where we were dug in. I immediately scrambled for my rifle, and George reached for his .45 automatic. He couldn't find his pistol, and on reaching for my own rifle, I found that it was frozen solid. I couldn't even stomp the bolt open with my foot, so George grabbed the Bazooka and we waited till they were almost on top of us when we both shouted, "Halt!" as loud as we could. Arms and weapons flew into the air as we caught them totally by surprise.

We moved them onto the roadway and George stood there covering them with his empty Bazooka, daylight streaming out of both ends of the empty weapon. I removed their gear and some helmets, and while we were doing this, others from our unit drifted over to us to oversee the proceedings. I had finished checking all of them, but there was one man wearing a camouflage suit and a peaked cap who, to me, seemed inordinately cocky. I decided to go over him again. This time I opened his outside suit and checked his uniform underneath. In an inside pocket I found a small .22 caliber automatic, often referred to as an escape pistol.

After we finished with prisoners, someone else took charge of them and George and I returned to getting the rest of our gear together. When we removed the raincoats from the bottom of the hole, George found his pistol. It must have slipped out of the holster during the night and had been hidden among the raincoats.

Black Holes in the Snow

After some time we were again ordered to prepare to move out. This time, instead of moving forward down the road, we moved in the other direction to where a sharp turn in the road brought us onto another road, which was the main roadway to the next village, the village of Mont le ban.

When we arrived on the lower road, there was again the usual waiting and milling around till things were organized. We were never sure why so much time was consumed in what always seemed such an elementary matter of simply moving forward. As was the case in so many previous occasions, this morning found us again gathering in small clusters of men, although we all knew better. There would always be the cry from one of the officers or noncoms, "Don't bunch up, one shell will get you all." There was a slight rise in the road ahead of us, and when several of us were together in front of the rise, mortar shells began dropping all around us. Dirty black holes began blossoming in the snow on every hand. Fred Dorsey was one of the first victims of that attack. We were all sickened to see Fred lying there beside one of those blackened holes in the snow in a grotesque posture of death, the ultimate humiliation.

In September, when I had returned to our unit from the hospital, it was positioned inside the Siegfried Line, just within the German border. I was warmly greeted by Fred Dorsey and Lester Fickel to a very depleted squad. They immediately began bustling around, getting together all the equipment I would need, and then went through the bed rolls on the rack on the back of the half-track to gather blankets for me. Because of the heavy casualties, there was always a surfeit of blankets and bedrolls. While I was organizing my equipment, I could hear Fickel and Dorsey inside the half-track. I soon understood that Fickel was reading one of the letters to Dorsey that Dorsey had just received from his wife. (Fred Dorsey could neither read nor write.)

I had decided that night to sleep underneath the half-track, and while I was arranging my blankets, I could hear the two of them having a mild argument. They were arguing about who they thought should be the next squad leader. Each one deferred to the other, saying that he should be the next one.

As I lay there underneath the half-track, the stillness of the night was suddenly rent by the long burst of fire from a nearby German machine gun that reverberated through the woods. That sound sent a chill up my spine, hearing that sound which I had not heard since Normandy. I was suddenly seized with an imminent and pervasive sense of encroaching hostility, not only because of that rapid firing machine gun, but now the trees and rocks and the very earth on which I lay also seemed to exude hostility, because I was inside the enemy camp. I was now on German soil.

Returning to combat the second time is far more difficult than that initial experience, because when I returned the second time, the incident in that narrow lane in Normandy had convincingly disabused me of the youthful illusion of invincibility, and just as quickly jarred me loose form the myth that "It won't happen to me." It was the warmth and friendliness of Dorsey and Fickel that helped me through the difficult transition of returning to combat. Now Fickel was gone, having been wounded a few days earlier and evacuated, and Dorsey lay dead in the snow.

The reaction to the mortar attack was immediate. Some of us made a break for a small copse about 200 yards to our right. Several of the tanks moved in that direction, so I made it a point to keep up with and beside one of them as a shield as I ran for the woods. There was a cattle fence hidden under the snow, and I caught my foot in it and went down. With Craig right behind me, I know I had at least one footprint in the middle of my back.

That mortar attack was so critical because it split the company. Only about fifteen of the Infantry made it to the woods. The others of our company had fallen back. This would separate us from the men I had been with constantly; Craig's was one of the few familiar faces.

Once inside the woods we settled down for another period of waiting. I was out of food and found a part of a loaf of hard, black German bread lying on the ground. It was not unusual to see German prisoners with a loaf of that bread simply strapped to their belts. As hungry as I was, it was too hard and sour to tempt me to more than a few bites, so I discarded it.

When the decision to move out came, we made ready, but as soon as the first tank began to move, there was an immediate response of direct fire from the village, either from tanks or from anti-tank guns. The tanks quickly retreated back into the woods. We could hear that there was an urgent conference taking place over the tank radios. The word was that there were Tigers in town. The Tiger tank was the most feared of all weapons in the German arsenal; like a tracked dreadnought, it was certainly the scourge of anything we possessed.

The call must have gone out for air support, because some time later a flight of P-47's arrived on the scene and, as was their custom, seemed to circle endlessly, but it was simply their way of carefully establishing the target. Once that was done, their execution was a wonder to watch. First, with their bombing runs, which on this occasion began directly overhead, the earth trembled with the impact of the detonating bombs that shook snow from the trees. Then during the strafing runs, again directly overhead, the planes themselves recoiled with the force of the eight .50 caliber machine guns, shattering the air with the fury of their bursts.

How many Tigers were involved, we did not know, but sometime later when another of our tanks moved, there was an immediate retaliation from the village, indicating that some of them were still alive and well.

As we sat there, crouched in the snow, waiting for a decision to be made, I happened to glance at a new young officer crouched nearby. I was taken aback by the look of fear that completely distorted his face. The baggage of fear is burdensome enough to carry, but when I looked at that young untried officer and realized that imposed upon him was also the responsibility of leadership, I felt a special measure of pity.

Since I was near the command tank, I could hear the urgency of the communication that was going on between our column and the higher command. By this time, the day was wearing on and darkness would soon cover the scene. It was then that we heard those infamous words over the radio, "You *will* move into that town!" Further, it was stated that there would be an artillery barrage lasting twenty minutes, after which we would be mounting the tanks and moving into the village.

There were three or four tanks in our detachment, formed in a single file inside the woods; one of them was a light tank, the others were Sherman tanks. When the barrage was just about over, we mounted the tanks. Three of us got aboard the light tank. This was my first experience with a tank other than the Sherman.

It was just about dark when the last shell of the barrage went crashing into the village. The tanks almost jumped out of the woods at the given signal, each one determined to outrun the other to the village. The three of us had quite a surprise when we saw how quickly the light tank outran the others. There was a stream midway between the woods and the village, but we were certain that our tank never touched the bottom of that creek bed. It simply leapt across.

The guns of all the tanks were firing, tracers pouring into the village, and by now, because of the superior speed of the lighter tank, the tracer bullets seemed to be passing us uncomfortably close as our tank moved farther ahead of the others. The commander of the tank on which we were riding did not raise his head above the turret; he just reached up to the .30 caliber machine gun above him, pointed it toward the village and fired what seemed to be one long, continuous burst. We were well in advance of the other tanks, and we could see that the driver was heading for the shelter of the nearest outbuilding.

We arrived there very quickly and the driver spun the tank to a halt behind a large shed. We had just hit the ground when the unexplainable happened; another barrage of artillery came in, and right on top of us. One man of the three that were on the tank took a large splinter of steel directly in the middle of his back and that finished him. The screams of the farm animals that had been caught in the intense fire of our approach were heartbreaking, as they charged around in complete terror, many of them no doubt wounded.

I immediately left the position where we had dismounted and made a run for the first house. A number of the houses in the village were already on fire, giving the night an eerie quality, with the sounds of the screaming animals and the somber sight of a town on fire.

A Loud, Horrible Scream

I entered the first house and since it faced away from the burning village, the interior of the house was extraordinarily dark. I shouted as I entered, but there was no response. It is amazing how fear heightens the senses, because I felt the presence of somebody in the room. I began probing around with the muzzle of my rifle and suddenly felt the unmistakable sensation of flesh. As my eyes grew more accustomed to the darkness, I saw the forms of two elderly people standing in front of me, too terrified to speak. I mumbled an apology to them and turned and left the house.

At this point I knew I was alone, but I was sure that as the others arrived, they too would begin moving immediately into the village. After leaving the first house I ran along some other buildings till I came to the gateway of a courtyard. Immediately inside the courtyard to the right of the entrance was a house with the top floor on fire. About six feet of the front of the house extended inside the courtyard, the remainder of the house was outside the courtyard. After entering through the gateway, I went around to the front door of the house and entered the open door. Directly inside, to the left, was the door to the cellar, which was also open. From the top of the narrow stairway that led to the cellar, I could see the glow of light.

Cautiously, I made my way down the steps and was surprised to see a number of candles setting on boxes with equipment that was unmistakably German, scattered around. (German equipment always had a very distinctive odor.) With this, I knew I was inside the German position. I returned up the stairs, and as I stood in the front door, I saw another gateway directly ahead of me across the courtyard. I then went forward along the other wall of the courtyard to the gateway and saw that it brought me out onto a street. At this time the air was alive with all kinds of sounds: the sound of heavy firing, the sound of tank engines everywhere, crackling flames, and still the shrieks of those terrified animals.

Directly across the street was a house, and for some reason I was contemplating making a run for that house. My mind was soon changed because directly from the other side of the wall, only a few feet from where I was standing, a machine gun opened up. The tracers from that gun were splattering off the wall of the house that moments before I had been planning to move toward. After the machine gun opened up, I decided to retreat back into the courtyard. I made my way through the rubble, and this time I went to the doorway of the other house that opened onto the courtyard, and stood in the doorway of the house to decide what to do next. When I made my way across the courtyard, I saw another American soldier enter the gateway that I had entered and stand in the shadows of that first house. Evidently there must have been enough light from the fires, when he entered, for him to recognize me as an American too, otherwise he would have probably fired, having taken me for a German soldier.

While I stood in the doorway, I saw two figures come to the entrance where I had just been moments before and pause to look, no doubt to investigate, because of the noise I had made moving through the rubble and broken glass. Since there were now two of us in the courtyard, I felt an added degree of confidence, so I shouted to the two figures in the gateway, "Kommen sie hier mit den handen hoche!" They paused for a moment. I shouted again, "Kommen sie hier mit den handen hoche!" This time I saw them raise their hands and move slowly toward me. The fires that were burning in the village made for an extremely confusing picture, because as the wind whipped the flames, the landscape would one moment be bright, and the next instant, as the flames died, the scene would again revert to the blackness of night.

As they approached me through the rubble-filled courtyard, I could see that their hands were raised. The American soldier, who was still standing in the shadows, made no move as I stepped out of the doorway to approach the two prisoners. So as I approached them, I was the only American involved in taking them prisoner, as far as they were concerned. The routine of taking prisoners during the last few weeks, some under the most unusual circumstances; some situations were almost comedic and would now prove almost fatal to me.

When I stepped in front of the first man, doing as I had done on so many previous occasions, I dropped my rifle to my left hand in order to remove any dangerous equipment. At that instant the prisoner made a movement and whether it was the result of that movement toward me or whether there was a glint of light from the fires around us, I saw that in his raised right hand there was a weapon. Since I was too close to him to bring my weapon to bear on him, I could do nothing but throw my rifle to the ground and, in doing so, disarm myself. I reached for his right hand with the weapon, to prevent him from bringing it down on me. I grabbed his hand with the pistol, and with my other arm, I grabbed him around his upper body. He, in turn, grabbed me around my upper body, and we tussled, trying to throw each other off balance. It was then that he fired his pistol and part of my hand went numb, nevertheless, I was still able to prevent him from bringing his arm down to where he could have done fatal damage. I could actually hear the other German soldier whimper with fear because of what was happening before him.

Meanwhile, for some reason, my companion did not move from his position, but remained hidden in the shadows, a fact that, without question, contributed to the whole unfortunate incident, since if he had moved forward and joined me, and the two German prisoners had been aware of the presence of both of us, nothing would have been attempted. In final desperation I shouted to my unknown companion, "For Pete's sake, give me a hand!" He moved forward toward us, and when he was upon my opponent, fired four shots. The German soldier gave a loud, horrible scream directly into my ear, and as the bullets struck home, he slipped from my grasp and crumpled to the ground at my feet. During the rapid sequence of action, the other German soldier somehow managed to flee into the darkness.

"Who is Roosevelt's Wife?"

The two of us made our way toward the gateway, and immediately after leaving the courtyard and moving a short distance, we were halted by a voice in the darkness. As the fires flared, we could make out the form of a Sherman tank ahead of us. I called out. "We're Americans, I'm hit. I want to get back!" The man in the tank did not believe that we were Americans, and the excited tone of his voice made me fear that we might yet be gunned down by our own men, but I persisted and said, "We're D Company, and we want to get back!" His next question was, "What's the password?" I replied that I didn't know, since we hadn't had one for quite a while. His doubts were still not satisfied, so in evident desperation he asked a question of last recourse that was probably asked many times before. "Who is Roosevelt's wife?" "Eleanor!" I replied. That satisfied him and we were finally permitted to pass through, back to our own position.

The guards were already in place outside the door of the first house we came to, so we entered and found that those inside, in that short time, had already set up; the room blacked out and the flickering light of candles throwing shadows around the room. The one sight that really astonished me was that of the imperturbable Craig, sitting on a chair with his feet propped up on a table as though the whole evening were just one great bore. There was an officer present, so I blurted out to him everything that had happened, explaining where this courtyard was and warning them that I was sure that there was a German tank on the other side of the wall of the courtyard, because, in thinking about it, I believed it was the machine gun from a tank that had fired when I attempted to cross that street.

Then I made a most foolish and shameful remark, a remark that was made in the stress of the moment. I said, "When you move up tomorrow and come to that courtyard, if that German soldier is still there, make sure that he's dead." Sometime later, I was told that when our unit moved up the next day, they did find the body of a soldier that turned out to be a German officer, and one of our men emptied his .45 into what was already a corpse. When he was reprimanded by the officer, he replied, "Kauffman told me to do it!"

There were already several wounded soldiers in the cellar of the house, so the officer told me to go down and join them, since there was a medic there to take care of my wound. I was given a shot of morphine by the medic and then he tried to put back in place a finger that was merely hanging on by the tendons. There was also a Belgian couple, who were assisting and scurrying around trying to help to make the men comfortable, in spite of the fact that, from what we gathered, they had lost a child as a result of our bombing. How magnanimous!

There was a considerable delay in bringing up the medical half-track to evacuate the wounded because of the heavy shelling that was going on, particularly in the area of a bridge and an intersection through which the half-track would have to pass.

When the medical half-track finally did arrive, we held our collective breaths till we finally got out of the danger zone. Being wounded, especially if it isn't of a real serious nature, actually brings a great sense of relief, since you've felt pretty certain that you were going to get it somehow.

When the waiting is over and you have survived, you experience a feeling akin to euphoria. Then our wounds were of no great concern to us.

Darkness to Light

One day as I walked down a large corridor in the hospital in Paris, I heard a very familiar voice say "Hi, Bob. I was expecting you." It was the voice of a friend of mine, Ross Overholt. We had become good friends in Germany while we were in the Scherpenseel area, where in comparing notes, we found an unusual similarity in our experiences. I had joined the 3rd Armored Division immediately following their first engagement in Normandy; Ross had joined a short time later. I was hit near St. Lo during the second week of July; Ross was wounded a few weeks later. We had both gone to different hospitals in England and had rejoined our unit just after it had crossed the German border in September. We also discovered that we both belonged to the same small Church denomination, although Ross lived in Michigan and I lived in Pennsylvania.

Although we were both nineteen years old, we would often have exceptionally good chats that were almost philosophical in their nature. On Christmas night in the Bulge, Ross had been wounded by the same shell that had killed both Lester Wertman and Lt. Mellitz, as well as wounding several others. Ironically, Ross was also wounded in the hand. So Ross evidently thought that since he had been hit, according to past performances, I should not be far behind, and the greeting I got, "I was expecting you," was an absolutely genuine reflection of the inevitabilities with which we lived.

In that village outside of Hebronval, when the house was struck by an artillery shell, and the scene that followed caused the new officer to ask the question, "What kind of men are you?" we had no illusions that we were a special breed of men. We knew that experience alone would reveal to him one of the great incongruities of war: that the very violence and horror of battle itself seemed to produce a mollifying agent that acted as a damper on the strings of the emotions. Were it not for that fact, the very force of the harshness and the severity of the conflict would agitate those strings with such intensity that the mind of a man would be shattered and shredded.

Seventy-two hours after the incident in the Belgian courtyard, lying in a Paris hospital, between something as unfamiliar as two white sheets, my experience was reminiscent of the Scriptural allegory of moving from the kingdom of darkness into the kingdom of light, since I had been transported from the dirt and death of the battlefield into the antiseptic serenity of a hospital room. However, it was then that the insulating protection of the mollifying agent began to dissolve, and as it did, and the sluice gates of my mind opened and the recollections of the recent past poured out, at night in the darkness of my room, I would lie in bed trembling, experiencing degrees of fear that I had not known before. We were not an unusual breed, just the most common among all men.

After leaving the hospital in Paris, before being transferred to England, I was moved to a hospital in what had been formerly the Normandy beachhead, to a place called Le Hay de Puits. In the hospital ward there was a phonograph, and one of the records that was played over and over again was a beautiful song with the cumbersome title, "Spring Will Be a Little Late This Year." For many of my fellow soldiers, that spring would never come; for others, spring would indeed be a little late; but for me, spring came just in time to end that bitter winter of my youth.

The End of the War

This second trip to the hospital lasted three months. As I was in
LeHavre on my way back to my unit, Germany surrendered and
the war in Europe came to an end. However, just because
Germany surrendered, the troops on the ground did not return
home immediately. I was able to rejoin my unit. The drama of
foxholes, going without sleep, and wondering if a German soldier
had you in his sights were now in the past. But there were still
things to do. For me the most important were simply to reestablish
old relationships and catch up with the events that I had 'thankfully'
missed. Then I was injured one last time. Nothing as significant
as an enemy bullet this time though. Just a vehicle accident. But
instead of a field hospital and waiting for the injury to heal so that I
could rejoin my unit, this time was I discharged and returned home
to the United States. Because of the discontinuity of my service
due to my several injuries, I was still a Private First Class. But I
was older and wiser in so many ways – ways that would help to
shape my life during the next 60+ years

Part II – People

A Soldier's Soldier

The barn where George Sampson won the "Silver Star"

George Sampson & myself

George Sampson died in November, 2007, at the age of eighty-nine. A lifelong resident of Allentown, PA, he was a steelworker in his youth, an operator of a vending machine business later on, a husband and a father. But there was also a time when George was a soldier, which is how I remember him best.

Our paths first crossed in Germany in late 1944, where the 36th Armored Infantry Regiment was then replenishing its depleted ranks following five months of combat. George was among a group of fresh replacements who were promptly trucked to a nearby quarry for additional weapons training, including test firing of the bazooka, after which he was assigned to 2nd Platoon, D Company. I had rejoined the platoon in September after recovering from wounds received in France, and George and I – a replacement and a combat veteran – were designated as the bazooka team for the newly reconstituted 3rd Rifle Squad. George was twenty-six, I was nineteen, and we were both PFC's.

Replacements typically met with a frosty reception for the simple reason that their inexperience usually resulted in a disproportionate number of casualties soon after they entered action. Few of us made an effort to get to know them until they had survived a few weeks at least. We went easier on newcomers to the war who showed confidence and personality, which described George exactly. Wiry and strong from his days at Bethlehem Steel, he combined physical presence with a workingman's relaxed sense of humor and a gift for storytelling, often ribald tales accompanied by tortured melodies from his harmonica. In my case acceptance came when I learned he was from Pennsylvania, just up the road from my hometown of Emmaus, and in fact had dated the sister of my best friend back home. It quickly seemed that I had known him forever.

George got his first taste of combat in the Battle of the Bulge, three weeks after he arrived, when 2nd Platoon walked straight into an ambush against elements of the 1st SS Panzer Division. Engulfed in a withering crossfire and commanded to withdraw, what was left of our platoon managed to crawl back down the hill and across an ice-cold stream under a blizzard of machine gun, grenade and mortar fire. What I recall from the incident is that George appeared unfazed by the torrential fire we had just escaped, but he was furious that we had been given so little information about the enemy's location and strength. It only made him madder when I told him that was how it was in combat, which he dismissed in unprintable language as simply not good enough. It was a telling moment, as it marked George as both brave and a thinker, the very qualities soldiers look to in a leader.

The Bulge campaign was waged in hundreds of villages and towns across the Ardennes, and at times it seemed that D Company had fought in all of them. It was also bitterly cold. At night, we looked for any building that would shelter us from the biting wind, but, as the bazooka team, George and I were often deployed ahead of the company, outside, where we dug-in along the road to intercept enemy tanks. Digging through the frozen earth was like chipping at concrete; when we had gone just deep enough and wide enough for both of us to sit down, we would lay our raincoats in the bottom of the hole for insulation, then climb in using my full-length overcoat to cover us. We took turns on watch, and though it was too cold to ever really sleep, we nonetheless were grateful for the hole.

One morning, about a month into the battle, we had emerged from yet another wretched hole and I was pounding on the overcoat, which had frozen like a plank overnight. I had propped my M-1 rifle against a tree while I attempted to loosen it up, when George whispered that an enemy patrol was approaching our position. He didn't have a rifle since he hauled the bazooka, but did carry a .45 caliber pistol, which, unbeknownst to George, had slipped from his holster during the night and was in the hole under the raincoats. Grabbing my rifle I pulled back on the bolt, but it too had frozen solid. By now the patrol was nearly on top of us. Seeing what was happening with me, unable to locate his .45, and with no time to load the bazooka, George raised the empty tube and shouldered it, daylight streaming from both ends. "Halt!" he hollered at the patrol with all his voice. "Halt!" Amazingly their hands flew into the air, and with my worthless rifle pointing at their chests, they were persuaded to drop their weapons. To this day I am convinced that George's quick thinking saved our lives. [see page 155 for more details on this story]

That night we got split up while clearing some houses, and I was wounded for the second time. Shipped out to England the next day, I did not rejoin 2nd Platoon until after Germany's surrender. I immediately went looking for George, who now was Staff Sergeant Sampson in charge of 2nd Squad. He was the same cheerful and uncomplicated man he was before, still spinning stories about this or that back home. Only later would I hear, and not from George, other stories that in my absence had earned him both the Silver and a Bronze Star for Valor.

We went home to Pennsylvania after the war, lived five miles from each other and got on with our lives. When his health began to fail in the last years of his life, we would meet for breakfast every other week, where the conversation invariably drifted back to that long ago time when we were soldiers. "You know," he said once, characteristically poking me on the arm as he spoke, "you and I are closer than brothers because of those days." He was right about that, and I've never received a finer compliment.

In life as in war there are those who just naturally stand out, men and women conspicuous for their actions and character regardless of what they do. George Sampson was one such person. As I watched him lowered into the ground on that cool November day, I could not help thinking that I belonged there with him, the two of us dug-in together one last time. A strange thought perhaps, but George would have understood it completely.

My Good Comrade Hans

German Cemetery

With Hans Zeplien

It may have been at one of the last Division Reunions that Colonel Lovelady attended that I had the pleasure of having a good conversation with him. We discussed the fighting in the "Stolberg Corridor," especially the offensive of November 16, 1944, that involved the heavy fighting around the villages of Werth, Scherpenseel and Hastenrath.

Several months later, I received a letter from a German historian, Gunter von der Weiden. Mr. von der Weiden informed me that my name had been submitted to him by Colonel Lovelady because of my interest in the "Stolberg Corridor." Gunter von der Weiden was in the process of writing a history of the fighting in that area since he was a citizen of Stolberg. In the course of our flood of correspondence, we became good friends and he had become simply, Gunter.

Gunter asked me to give my recollections of my participation in the fighting in the offensive of November 16th. I made a tape recording of my experiences and that tape recording became a 32-page transcript.

Enter Hans Zeplien

At the same time that Gunter received my communication, which was translated into German, he also had the diary of Hans Zeplien, who as a 1st LT., commanded the 14th Anti-Tank Company of the 89th Regiment, 12th Volksgrenadier Division. Gunter gave my copy to Hans, and in turn, I received the English translation of the diary of Hans Zeplien. This began an incredible three way communication.

In the spring of 1990, I had decided to take a trip to Europe, inviting two good friends to join me, Alan Fleming, a near relative and also a TV producer at our area TV channel, and Pete Derr. When we arrived in Germany, my friend Gunter said that he had tried to arrange a meeting between Hans and me, but something developed and the meeting was canceled. Again, in 1993, I planned another trip to Europe with Alan Fleming, with the purpose of video-taping as much of the trip as possible. We would be meeting in the very same setting where we had met before as enemies, the village of Scherpenseel, and the irony was that we met in the house of two of my dear German friends, Martin and Katie Artz. The Artz house was a house we had taken and occupied for a short time when Scherpenseel was taken on November 17th. The room in which we met had had, in 1944, the barrel of a .30 caliber machine gun sticking out of the front window, facing a ridge which was still occupied by the Germans.

The Handshake

Meeting Hans was a real joy. He too is the consummate historian. He came armed with a whole array of documents from every area of his service as both a Non-Commissioned and a Commissioned Officer. We sat at the table for about 45 minutes when Hans simply paused, laid his hand on my arm and very matter of fact-like said, "Robert, I like you." It was truly the beginning of a wonderful friendship. With that auspicious beginning, we spent the remainder of the day touring part of the battlefield, along with his dear wife. We concluded a beautiful, but exhausting day with a delightful dinner in a most charming restaurant.

In the early part of 1994, I received a letter from a Josef Schwagerl who lived near Munich. I was surprised to find an invitation to a reunion of the 12th Volksgrenadier Division to be held in Merode, Germany in the Fall of the year. It was a distinct honor; however, having just been to Europe the previous year, I didn't think it feasible to incur the expense of another trip so soon. Sadly, I had to decline the invitation. However, several weeks later I received a letter from my friend Gunter. In his letter, was also a translated letter from my good friend, Hans. In his letter, Hans made the most astonishing offer. He said that if I would agree to come to the reunion, he would assume all of the expenses of the trip because he wanted me there. It was an offer that I could not decline.

In the fall of 1994, Alan and I flew to Europe and met my friend Hans in Scherpenseel. We then traveled to Merode, the scene of the reunion. Hans saw to it that our accommodations were all first class. I must admit that my first experience with this group of veterans from the 12th Volksgrenadier Division was rather intimidating. I did not know how the individual German veterans felt about my presence, in view of the fierce combat that our two Divisions had participated in. In fact, with all of the combat experience that my friend Hans had in the fighting in Europe, he astonished me when he told me that the fighting in the "Stolberg Corridor," was the fiercest fighting that he had experienced. I was certain that he would have said the fighting in Russia was worse, especially in the Demyansk "Kessel".

The Reunion and a Man Named Hess

The first meeting that Alan and I attended was, to say the least, very interesting. My understanding of the German language is minimal, but there were bits and pieces that I could understand. What did not surprise me was the fervor of their singing and, instead of clapping, the pounding on the table. Across the table from me was a very friendly and interesting veteran. His name was Hess. His Regiment had fought opposite the 9th Infantry Division. He told me about a fierce fight they had with a small patrol that entered their lines. The man next to him was shot in the face, and one American fell near him, having also been shot in the head.

After the Americans were driven back, Hess said that his Company Commander ordered him and another man to go forward and retrieve the body of the fallen American. When they dragged the body back to their position, they checked the body for identification and the personal items found on him. He had a pack of Lucky Strike cigarettes and a photo of himself with either his wife or girlfriend. His name was Swenson. The two were then ordered to bury the American soldier. They dug the grave and buried him and fashioned a cross from some ammunition boxes with his name identified on the cross. Hess urged me to try to find the family and tell them that their family member was treated with great respect. After much searching, I located the family and wrote a letter to them, telling them of the experience that this former German soldier had related to me. I included a statement by the German soldier, Hess. The response that I and Hess received was cold and without any sense of gratitude for what this German soldier had done, as well as for his long concern over the years that Swenson's family might know how he met his end and was respectfully treated, even in death. I was deeply offended by the cold display of ingratitude for what the German soldier had done.

The Memorial Services

There is a Castle in Merode, and once a year the Chapel is opened to the Division for its Memorial Service. It was a very moving experience to see our former enemy grieve for their own dead, and the pain that still remained. This was repeated over and over again as we visited various memorials and cemeteries. There was an especially moving tribute held in a forest outside of the city of Duren. The city had sustained very heavy civilian casualties because of the numerous bombing raids.

Allan and I were with Hans as he visited several cemeteries where his very own men, from the company he commanded, were buried. To see Hans go through that very difficult personal grief was, for us, also a painful experience. Knowing him, he was probably wondering whether he had done everything that he could have done as a Company Commander, to save the lives of his men.

The Return to Scherpenseel

It was indeed an honor to have been invited to the 12th VG Division Reunion and to share the common experience of soldiers: the pride of accomplishment and the pain and grief for those of our comrades who were lost. Those feelings are not only the prerogatives of the victor, but also of the vanquished.

When Alan and I joined Hans in our trip back to Scherpenseel, it was with the purpose of video-taping as much as we could of the recollections that Hans had of his participation in the heavy fighting that took place in the infamous "Stolberg Corridor." One of the first places we visited was the building in Hastenrath that served as his Command Post. It happened to be the cellar of the priest's home, adjacent to the church in the village. Hans told of the heavy shelling by the American artillery and how he would have to return to Regt. Hqts for his instructions and orders, the whole time running the gauntlet of artillery fire. His travels back to Regiment were by bicycle, and he showed us the place where he parked his bike before making a dash for the CP.

Commanding an Anti-Tank Company gave Hans a large area of responsibility in forming an anti-tank defense against the offensive that the Germans knew was coming. He drove us around the perimeter of his defense responsibility, and it was considerable. Not only did he position and control the 7.5 guns, but also the Rocket Projectors as well as the one-man Panzerfaust.

When the 3rd Armored, along with the 1st and 9th Infantry Divisions, crossed the German border south of Aachen, both the German and American forces were exhausted from heavy casualties and worn out tanks and other vehicles, There was no question that it would take considerable time until our forces were reconstituted and brought up to strength. A strong American offensive, the Germans knew, was inevitable. The fact that it would take two months to make it possible, gave the Germans that much time to prepare for the coming attack, and when you give the

Germans that much time to prepare, you are going to pay a terrible price. We learned that painful lesson in the Normandy hedgerows where we met the German defensive skill. And even though the forces under the command of 1st Lt. Hans Zeplien were severely depleted, not only in men, but also equipment, the defensive lessons learned on the Russian front would be to the detriment of our own 3rd Armored Division tankers.

Hans Prepares for the Attack

Before the November 16th attack, Hans would make the rounds at night to visit every man and every position so that in two nights he would cover his entire defensive position. There were areas where the ground was marshy and the foxholes would soon fill with water. Wood was brought forward to place in the bottom of the holes to give some comfort to the men occupying those positions. October was an unusually rainy month, to which our unit could attest. This did not bode well for the coming attack, especially with the difficulty of negotiating soft ground on the narrow tracks of our Sherman tanks.

At the very same time, our own company was positioned within yards of the German positions; in fact, we were so close that we could hear the horse and wagon that would bring the soldiers their one hot meal every evening. We could actually hear the sound of the mess kits as the German soldiers ate. The same could not be said about our own unit. No hot meals were ever brought forward to us.

When the attack was launched on November 16, preceded by a horrific artillery barrage, the Germans were well prepared to meet it. Belton Cooper, in his book "Death Traps," gives us the gory details of our tank losses, just incredible losses of men and material. Another excellent account of the attack comes from Lt. Earle, who commanded the lead Sherman tank. Earle's account of his experience inside the tank is probably one of the most graphic descriptions of what it is like to sustain hits from anti-tank guns. Needless to say, the attack did not achieve the breakthrough that was anticipated.

Hans Zeplien and Oliver Wiggs

In the Fall of 1994, as Hans and I toured the battlefield we came to a point that overlooked the large sugar beet field that proved a real killing ground for the German anti-tank forces. Hans pointed to the distant corner of the large field where the villages of Scherpenseel and Hastenrath meet. He then told me the most astonishing story. He said that after dark, on the night of the 16th, he took another man with him to check out the remaining positions. He said that suddenly, in the darkness, he heard the sound of tank engines coming to life. He could tell by the blue flames of the exhausts that there were three tanks that began a run across the large field, heading for the village of Werth. He and the other man immediately took out after the three tanks, Hans carrying a Panzerfaust. However, Hans said that the tanks began moving too fast, and they were unable to catch up in order to fire the Panzerfaust.

Some years earlier I had met a man who lived in the same town as I. His name was Oliver Wiggs. I had seen his name mentioned in our Division publication and saw that he lived in Emmaus. We had great visits together. In his later years he and his wife moved to a retirement home. After his dear wife died and he was no longer able to drive, I would take him on shopping excursions. He was always a natty dresser and a lover of fine tobacco.  During one of our visits together he began talking about his experiences in the war, and the November 16 attack came up. Oliver was in I Co. 33rd Regt., the same company as Lt. Earle. He spoke of the heavy casualties that they had sustained and said that their attack across the large sugar beet field ended at the juncture of the villages of Scherpenseel and Hastenrath where they were surrounded by German Infantry. Wiggs left the tank to fight more effectively, in the course of which he won the Silver Star for gallantry. There were only three tanks that survived that fateful attack. Since the three tanks were low in ammunition and without infantry support, the three tank commanders decided to make a run across the large field for the village of Werth.

Can you imagine my complete surprise when Hans fully confirmed the story of Oliver Wiggs. I was fortunate to get these two men together, so when Oliver and I would finish a shopping tour we would end up in a Red Lobster restaurant where we would end the meal with a toast to Hans. We would have a waiter or waitress photograph the toast, and I would mail a copy to Hans. In one of the last letters that I received from Hans before Oliver died, Hans said that I should tell Oliver that the next time he wouldn't chase him with a Panzerfaust; instead he would chase him with a bouquet of flowers. What a tribute to the beautiful spirit between these two former enemies.

Hans and Lynn Haufschild

In the late eighties, I received a letter from a man by the name of Lynn Haufschild, from Madison, South Dakota. He had read an article that I had written for our Division publication, concerning the fighting around Werth, Scherpenseel and Hastenrath. He told me that his brother William was killed on November 17 in Hastenrath. He also told me that his brother was a member of "F" Co. of the 33rd Regt. He asked me if I could help find out where and how his brother was killed. During my visit to Scherpenseel with Hans, I placed the issue before him, and he determined where Lynn's brother's tank must have been and that, in all probability, his brother was killed outside of his tank by German Infantry.

There is a school house at the juncture of those two villages, and it was used by the Germans as an excellent observation post. At the time of the fighting there, we were amazed at the accuracy of their artillery and mortar fire, until we realized the perfect picture that the observation post gave them. We ascertained that William Hausfchild died about a hundred yards in front of the school building.

I put Lynn Haufschild in touch with my friend Hans and another good friendship developed. They had good communications, including telephone calls. When Lynn Haufschild and his wife celebrated their 50th wedding anniversary, Hans sent them a congratulatory card with a generous sum of money enclosed. This is another example of what a great man Hans is. To me, his kindness and generosity are without parallel. That is why I am honored to call him, my good comrade Hans.

Other People

I was able to make several trips to Europe many years later - visiting some of the significant places of my service and meeting others who had connections through those events of the 1940's. Rather than write about them, I share here a number of pictures of these places and people.

1 – the corner of basement foundation in Mrs. Gaby's house where I was when artillery was called down on our own position

2 – German historians – Gunter von der Weiden, myself, unidentified, Heino Brandt

3 – with dear German, Scherpenseel friends, Martin & Kati Artz

4 – beloved Belgian friend, Jose Burnotte, now deceased

5 – German and Belgian historians: son Alan, Albert Schulte, Timm Haasler, me, Eddy Monfort, Bernard Lambert

6 – with invaluable Belgian friends: Mr. & Mrs. Franz Dester and son Nicolas

7 – with wonderful Belgian friends: Roger & Madeline and her brother, Jose Burnotte

8 – with a wonderful and unique Belgian historian and a true friend and Belgian gentleman, Andre Hubert

9 – shrapnel in the church pew in the Grandmenil church from the blast that George Sampson and I had fired as our squad Bazooka team

10 – the blanket which is the backdrop for this montage is that in which Claudine Lambert was held as a 19-month old infant when

she was severely wounded by a German grenade. The shrapnel is also seen here.

11 – with dear Scherpenseel friends, Marita & Martin Esser

12 – with delightful Scherpenseel friends, Willie, Monica, Dorchan and very close and dear friend Otmar Rehfisch.

13 – with Mr. and Mrs. Raymond Geome, two very important Belgian friends. It was he who introduced me to Major General Michael Reynolds, whose friendship has been invaluable and inspirational.

14 – with Geoffrey Mapstone, whom I have known as a very young lad when I was invited into the warmth of the Mapstone home during those pre D-Day times.

15 – one of the thirteen German tanks that bypassed twelve infantrymen and one Sherman tank on the morning of December 26th

16 – Alan Fleming, my traveling companion on five trips to Europe, ensconced in the historic Glastonbury chair, used for important ritual functions

17 – with Roger & Renee Burnotte, owners of le val d'Hebron, hotel in Hebronval. To our most generous and lovable hosts during all of our visits to Belgium, our eternal gratitude.

18, 19, 20, 21 – two purple hearts for wounds received in Normandy and the Bulge, the Bronze Star for Meritorious Achievement in ground combat, and the coveted Combat Infantry Badge

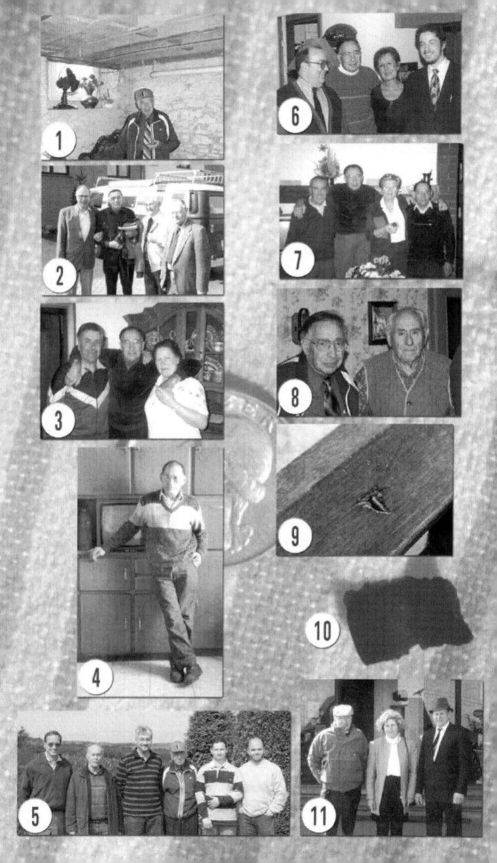

Part III – Remembrance

The Normandy Cemetery

Normandy Cemetery

With son Alan

In the early part of 1999, my sister Dolly and my brother-in-law, Gerald, asked me to take them to Europe to visit the places where I had been during the war. They wanted to do this to celebrate their fiftieth wedding anniversary. Since I had already made eight previous trips to Europe, this posed no problem.

During the time of making our plans, I spoke with a good friend of mine, Greg Heilman, who is an avid student of history, telling him of our plans. Greg has a dear aunt, Betty Thompson, whom I had met several years earlier. Betty Thompson had lost her young husband on Omaha Beach on D-Day. It was decided that during our stay in Normandy, we would visit the grave of that young husband, Donald Weisel.

In the fall of 1999, we flew to Brussels, and then drove to the Ardennes, the scene of the Battle of the Bulge, and visited various places there and also visited with my very dear Belgian friends. As I had done on previous visits, we also drove to the Henri-Chapelle Cemetery where, of all the cemeteries, most of my friends and comrades from our unit are buried. We then drove to Germany to visit some equally beloved German friends.

We drove from Germany to Normandy, to Bayeux and stayed in an old Norman manor owned by a retired British Colonel and his wife. I had stayed there on a previous visit to Normandy. We stopped in Bayeux at a floral shop where I purchased a single red rose to place on the grave of Donald Weisel, thinking that would be more eloquent. From there we drove to the Normandy Cemetery. We were very fortunate in having a very vivacious and articulate young French lady as our guide. Because of the size of the cemetery, she drove us to the grave site in her car. She had with her two flags, a small American flag and also a small French flag, along with a Polaroid camera.

As we stood and knelt by the grave of Donald Weisel, she placed the flags beside the cross and I laid that solitary rose on his grave. The young lady then took a photograph of that scene for the next of kin, Betty Thompson, which is a custom that the cemetery officials observe. The young lady then proceeded to give us some information about the cemetery, some of which I had known, but some information I had not heard before. I knew that there were over 9,000 young Americans buried there, but I was shocked when she told us that there were 38 sets of brothers buried there, and there are 33 sets of brothers buried side by side. That really cut me to the quick because my own dear wife lost two young brothers in that war; one with the First Division in North Africa, and the other on a destroyer off of Okinawa. The forward gun turret in which he was serving was struck directly by a Kamikaze, and there was nothing of him ever recovered, even for burial.

As we left the gravesite, I walked among the crosses and struggled with so many emotions. I thought of those 9,000 crosses, and then

I thought of all of the blessings I have enjoyed. I remembered that the cemetery in Normandy should be my present address. I thought of how God had blessed me with over 55 additional years of life and how He had blessed me with a lovely wife, three handsome children and eight wonderful grandchildren. I then multiplied 9,000 crosses times 50 years and came to the staggering sum of 450,000 unlived years represented by those crosses. 450,000 unlived years with all of the incredible potential of each life and each year. What a staggering thought!

There was something else that truly puzzled me and that was the question of why of all the cemeteries that I had visited, especially the Henri-Chapelle Cemetery, did my visit to the Normandy Cemetery evoke such a strong emotional response? After much thought, something occurred to me: the cemetery at Henri-Chapelle lies in a setting of almost perfect peace and tranquility. It seems as though even the birds whisper when they fly overhead. But not Normandy. I concluded that the great difference is the waves, the sound of those waves, the unrelenting sound of those waves as they wash ashore at Omaha Beach.

I thought of the young man whose grave we had just visited and then I thought of my own life in comparison, with all of the many many blessings that have accrued to me over these more than fifty-five additional years. It was then that those waves seemed to have a very stern and a very severe and profound personal message to me; a stern reminder and a very severe warning for me to never, ever forget the magnitude of the sacrifice that young man made.

It then seemed that each wave as it moved toward the shore, still carried with it all of the horror and all of the terror of the last few moments of that young man's life, and each wave had the sound of a bell tolling out another and another and another of his unlived years. And each succeeding wave carried the painful reminder that the young man buried up there on that bluff overlooking Omaha Beach, unlike me, would never ever know the fathomless pride of fathering a precious son or daughter. And each succeeding wave was a reaffirming reminder that the young man buried up there beneath that gleaming, white marble cross, unlike me, would never achieve the blessings of old age, and unlike me, he would never, ever enjoy the profound experience of just holding and hugging and kissing a beloved grandson or granddaughter.

And then I saw a wave, and borne on its crest were the scattered petals of a crushed rose -- the painful, painful remembrance of the anguish of that wounded and broken heart of the young, loving wife that would never mend. And as those waves came sweeping in toward that shore, they each gently and reverently kissed the sands of that beach, because, to me, those waves represented the tears of a nation weeping for its young. And the unrelenting sound of those waves is God's eternal reminder of the enormity of the price that was paid for our freedom and for my freedom and privilege to stand here. And in standing here, I would like to cry out to all of those dear young men, "Yes, you were robbed, indeed, you were robbed of the most sublime gift that we possess; you were robbed of your very lives; but, dear young men, we too were robbed; we were robbed of you; and we were robbed of your love; and we were robbed of your dreams and your hopes and your aspirations."

"And yes, dear young men, we were also robbed of those thousands of precious sons and daughters that you never had the privilege to father, and who would have borne the very image of your greatness. And we were also robbed of those thousands of beloved grandsons and granddaughters who would never know the magnitude of your sacrifice. Yes, we were all robbed by that insidious thief called war."

But then I wondered, what more could I say to Betty Thompson and my own dear wife who have suffered such terrible loss, except to repeat to them the words to an anthem for which those young men died:

"Oh beautiful, for heroes proved
in liberating strife,
who more than self their country loved,
and mercy more than life.
America, America,
God shed his grace on thee,
and crown thy good with brotherhood
from sea to shining sea."

Index

Made in the USA
Charleston, SC
17 May 2010